태 권 도

TAE KWON DO

The Indomitable Martial Art of Korea

BASICS, TECHNIQUES, AND FORMS

GRANDMASTER
Dong Keun Park
&
MASTER
Allan Schein

Invisible Cities Press
41 Northfield Street
Montpelier, VT 05602
www.invisiblecitiespress.com

Cataloging-in-Publication Data available from the Library of Congress

ISBN 1-931229-46-5

Anyone practicing the techniques in this book does so at his or her own risk. The
authors and the publisher assume no responsibility for the use or misuse of information contained in this book or for any injuries that may occur as a result of practicing
the techniques contained herein. The illustrations and text are for informational purposes only. It is imperative to practice these holds and techniques under the strict
supervision of a qualified instructor. Additionally, one should consult a physician
before embarking on any demanding physical activity.

Printed in the United States

Book design by Peter Holm, Sterling Hill Productions
Edited by Carmine Grimaldi

DEDICATIONS

Grandmaster Park

I would like first and foremost to thank God for all His blessings and consistent guidance.

To my parents, Park, Sung Joong and Oh, Jong Rye who are forever in my heart and an integral part of my spirit.

I'd like to dedicate this book to my wife, Lisa (Young Ju), who embodies strength, support, faith, courage, endurance, laughter and love. To my children, John and Jane, may our journey lead them to their own destinies filled with peace, prosperity and love.

Lastly, gratitude to Grandmaster Chong Woo Lee and Allan Schein with whom this book came into being.

Master Schein

I dedicate this book to my loving, supportive and wonderful parents, Max and Ethel Schein. They taught me to believe in myself, to have confidence, and they showered me with unconditional love. They taught me many of the important lessons in life: to finish what I start; to do things right the first time; the importance of family and friends; how to learn; common sense; self-reliance; loyalty; humor; and love.

I would also like to thank Grandmaster Park and Master John Park for their invaluable knowledge and technical input throughout the production of this book. The opportunity of working with, and learning from, one of the all time greats has been a pleasure and a privilege. My sincerest thanks also go to the many talented students and Masters from the DK Park School that performed to perfection throughout the photo shoot as models. Their excellent technique, generosity of time, support for the process and patience with the technical aspects is greatly appreciated. Without you all, this book would not have achieved our desired level of excellence. Special thanks goes to Master Mike Palumbo, who gave me a gift I can never adequately repay. He is my teacher, my friend, and my buddy.

Models appearing are listed alphabetically:

Antonio Anazco
Sonny Candelaria
Timothy Colanta
Craig Coletta
Maria Joanna Cuyson
Russell Isaacson
Philip Lo
Dan Mackle
Theodore Moschovas
Abdalla Mostafa
Steve Nalley
Kensuke Okabayashi
Master Mike Palumbo
Grandmaster Dong Keun Park
Master John Park
Master Allan Schein
Reena Singh
Tina Singh
Master Lesley Thompson

All techniques were photographed at the DK Park Taekwondo School located at 32 Journal Square, Jersey City, New Jersey.

Photos by Boston area photographer Leonard J. Eisenberg.
Archive photos ©D.K. Park, all rights reserved.
Additional photos courtesy David and Amy Johnson and
    William Happel.

TABLE OF CONTENTS

TECHNIQUES

Great Grandmaster Chong Woo Lee

Dear Readers,

First, I would like to congratulate Grandmaster Dong Keun Park for publishing his first book on Taekwondo. I was thrilled, excited and very glad, when I heard from Park that he would write a book on this martial art.

Park was one of the outstanding students under my instruction in the early birth of the modern Taekwondo. Not only was he well known as the undefeated champion for over 6 1/2 years of competition in Korea, he was also a dedicated and hard-working young martial artist. He showed his leadership among his peers. Above all, his good friendship and help to others were his best assets. These are character traits that every martial arts student should learn. I believe that Park is the best model for anyone who wants to be a true martial artist.

I can honestly say that this book is the culmination of DK Parks philosophy in the martial art and the way of wisdom. The book is filled with rich resources of Taekwondo gathered from over 50 years of his experience in the martial art. It is simply invaluable to any martial art instructors and students who are interested in learning not only Taekwondo but also other martial arts as well.

As it is the case in any other martial art, it is crucial and very imperative for a student to learn the basic skills in a right way. This book teaches and guides you in every necessary basic and advanced techniques in detail. It is well explained and illustrated with quality pictures and articulated instructions. Remember that you can not learn Taekwondo just by reading it; you must practice it with your body. This book will also ensure that you are able to develop more advanced techniques of your own later on. I truly hope that you will not only learn Taekwondo itself but also the Way of Wisdom, together.

Again, it is my honor and great pleasure that I heartily endorse this fine Taekwondo book to you as a reference and training book, without any reservation.

Great Grandmaster Chong Woo Lee
Jido Kwan Tae Kwon Do

INTRODUCTION

EEEYYYYYAAAAAAAAAHHHHHHHHHHHHHH!!! What a thrill it is for us to hear the scream of combat in a martial arts movie. It's unmistakable, exhilarating, and a sure sign of action. There probably isn't a kid anywhere in America who doesn't recognize or use that call. It's everything it promises to be. It's a call to action, a cry of battle, and the sound of an indomitable spirit. We all know what it means, but do we really know what it takes to reach the point where that one cry will define years and decades of study and practice? Of course, it looks great when it's shown in the movies. But these high kicks and flying techniques, achieved after many years of regimented training, are the distinct moves and actions that define Tae Kwon Do, separating it from all other martial arts. It is particularly distinguished by its flying kicks, which were originally designed to knock a man off a horse, hurt a man in armor or to close distance rapidly and with great power. These are the ancient moves of the Hwarang and Subaki warriors, re-taught by Masters over generations, preserved, refined, and now spread throughout the entire modern world.

As authors of a book on Tae Kwon Do, we are humbled by the vast history and considerable documentation available to anyone interested. The internet has become a marvel of information availability, with accessible sites for the World Taekwondo Federation, Kukkiwon, Tae Kwon Do Hall of Fame, numerous school systems and individual schools, as well as resources for equipment, books and magazines, forms, DVD's and videos. You should take advantage of these resources, and explore online photo files for some fabulous pictures of Tae Kwon Do in action.

There have been numerous books written on Tae Kwon Do, some of them delving into detail about getting started, or describing the history of Tae Kwon Do and Korea, or even books covering just two or three fighting forms. This book will not attempt to cover all the material that can be compiled about Tae Kwon Do, but rather will start with a basic introduction to the many areas of application. After, we will portray kicking techniques and their progressions, self defense and sparring techniques, and all primary patterns from white belt through black belt. Crisp color digital photography will clearly and fully show you the details and progression of each technique. Tae Kwon Do is not an art you can fully teach yourself. You will require instruction, and rather than include every stretch and warm-up exercise that so many books show, we will trust your instructors to guide you on many class basics. This volume will describe, and then visually show, how to use your hands and feet as weapons, along with how to perform the various kicks, punches and stances. Then we will combine these elements, adding specific techniques in a natural progression up through the belt ranks to first degree black belt. Reliable, well-trained professional instructors are available in most every city and town in America. It is now relatively easy to locate a school and take the action necessary to create a Tae Kwon Do learning experience for you and your family. Starting to learn Tae Kwon Do is as easy as showing up at a school. So if you've been thinking about it, thinking about learning how to defend yourself, or wanting to get in better physical condition, take action. And get started. Our goal in writing this book is to allow people to learn more about this valuable and practical Korean martial art, and take their first steps by reading through this beginning guide. By acquiring the knowledge contained within its pages, you will have the ability to better defend yourself and your loved ones.

GRANDMASTER DONG KEUN PARK

9th Dan Black Belt, Lifetime Undefeated Champion Fighter,
and Coach of Champions.

Legends are larger than life, and few true living legends walk this planet. Grandmaster Dong Keun Park is such a man, and the stories, history and accomplishments of his life are as rich in fact as the movies we love are filled with fantasy. He is a leader in every sense of the word; from his intimate involvement with a lifetime of Tae Kwon Do competition, to his position as head coach of US Olympic and National teams, and as an active member of his Korean community both in the greater New York and New Jersey region, as well as nationally. Yet, he remains unaffected by his astounding successes and is a spiritual, humble and truly genuine individual.

As a young boy, his parents' home was burnt to the ground and they found it necessary to go into hiding during this time of war. They brought Dong Keun Park to a Bhuddist monastery to be sheltered while they were forced to seek refuge elsewhere. At this monastery, he learned and refined his abilities and gained his skills in the Korean martial art of Tae Kwon Do. His training was traditional and intense in ways that Americans never get to experience. He trained outdoors in grassy fields, and in the mud when the weather was poor. In winter, he often trained in snow, always barefoot and wearing only gloves and the traditional Dobok (training uniform). Through experimentation, and trial and error, he developed techniques used and seen by few other Tae Kwon Do stylists. He incorporated these techniques in creating a truly unique fighting style. Grandmaster Park is of the order of Ji Do Kwan, the true and dominant fighters among this art in the years before it was incorporated with the other Kwans to form what was then the newly named art of Tae Kwon Do. When still a young man, he gained a position on the Republic of Korea's (South Korea) National team. He is a legendary champion, competing in more than 200 championship bouts, winning them all without ever having lost a fight. Most of his victories were won by knockout. He dominated the international competition for $6\frac{1}{2}$ years, and remains a lifetime undefeated champion. He retired from the national team while still a young man, partly to allow others a chance at achieving championship status, and partly to advance to the next phase of his amazing career. Upon retirement from the competition ring, he was immediately inducted into the Korean Tae Kwon Do Hall of Fame. He was the complete and consummate martial artist, excelling not only as a fighter, but also in breaking techniques, weapons knowledge and use, and real life self-defense techniques. He was the complete warrior and leader, and the ideal that every other martial artist strived to become.

Shortly after his retirement from the national team, he was offered an incredible honor and opportunity. Upon personal request from the king of Thailand, Grandmaster Park relocated to Bangkok with his family. He had been asked by the king to teach Tae Kwon Do to the royal family and the American military. He brought Tae Kwon Do to Thailand, where it has grown, as it has worldwide, to be a dominant art.

Grandmaster Park came to the United States in 1970, and for his first year taught Tae Kwon Do from a rented two car garage in Jersey City. He opened his formal school in Jersey City, New Jersey, on September 1, 1971, where it remains today, but at its second location in Journal Square. He built it into one of the most prominent schools ever to grace American soil. In the year of his arrival, he was already achieving recognition throughout America, and appeared several times on the Johnny Carson show. He thrilled audiences coast to coast with his amazing performances and seemingly super-human demonstrations of Tae Kwon Do techniques. Americans already had some awareness of Tae Kwon Do. But this was a time of redefining the identity of American youth, and Grandmaster Park, along with other newly arrived Masters, were an integral part of that redefined image. Baby boomers, and the younger generations, flocked to his school and others around the nation with a thirst for knowledge that helped assure Tae Kwon Do's future in America forever.

By 1975, Grandmaster Parks' students had achieved national and international notoriety by competing and successfully winning medals for the first USA National Tae Kwon Do team and at the Second World Tae Kwon Do Championships in Seoul Korea, both in 1975. The legend continued to grow.

In his personal life, Grandmaster Park remembered his friends and old teammates from his days on the Korean national team. During his first ten years in America, there were always friends and juniors living in the Park household who he assisted by giving them their chance at success here in America. He was a mentor, benefactor and brother to these men, openly offering his friendship, loyalty and generosity while asking nothing tangible in return.

Having fully established himself as an accomplished coach with his own internationally winning students, Grandmaster Park went on to become head coach for the US Team in the Third World Championships in Stuttgart, Germany in 1979. In 1982, he was named Coach of the Year by the A.A.U. (the Amateur Athletic Union, forerunner to the USTU, the United States Taekwondo Union). From 1982 through 1996, he was the Chairman of the Coaching Committee of the USTU. He was Head Coach of the 1992 U.S. Olympic team, and the most winning coach of the U.S. Olympic Festival from 1988 to 1992. He coached Herb Perez to a Gold Medal at the Barcelona Olympiad in 1992. He also coached Lynette Love, the four-time world champion, including her gold medal performances in the 1988 and 1992 Olympiads.

In 1993 he was head coach for the US World Championship team, which competed in New York City. In 1994 he was head coach for the

Goodwill Games in St. Petersburg, Russia. The list of champions he encouraged and taught is too long to list, but he has been a man of great influence and inspiration for many of America's Tae Kwon Do greats.

Grandmaster Park was named Tae Kwon Do Times Man of the Year in 1997.

He was inducted into the Tae Kwon Do Times Hall of Fame in 1998.

He was inducted into the Tae Kwon Do Hall of Fame in 1999.

He was inducted into the Living Legends Hall of Fame in 2005.

Although he has retired from active coaching, he still teaches at the Jersey City Dojang, and is still extremely active in the Tae Kwon Do community worldwide. The lessons he has taught others are still being passed on through his students and the champions he has taught and coached. He has taught more than 2,000 black belts. He is also an accomplished golfer and businessman. He is an active member of the Korean Professional Golf Association (KPGA). As a businessman, he was the successful importer of the wonderfully flavorful and highly favored Korean barley liqueur known as Soju, and O.B. Beer. His New Jersey school is still prominent today under the daily direction of his very capable and talented son, Master John Park. John Park is himself a highly successful and prominent Tae Kwon Do competitor, instructor and coach, having personally taught and coached several hundred notables in the Tae Kwon Do community. Master John is also a member of the Tae Kwon Do Hall of Fame, and a respected and prominent member of our national Tae Kwon Do community.

A Living Legend

First as a great champion, then as a great coach, Grandmaster Park's legacy will endure and inspire others for generations to follow. His winning techniques and the wisdom printed between the covers of this book are only a small part of the complete living encyclopedia of knowledge and experience that is Dong Keun Park. He is among the best known, most respected, and highly regarded of the world's Grandmasters. He has fought with the best and beaten them all. He has coached the best, and led them to the top of the championship podium. He is a humble man who has given more than he ever asked in return. It is with the greatest respect and humility, and my sincerest appreciation that I have been granted the exceptional honor of working as his co-author. We hope you find this book a valuable and useful tool and guide. Welcome to our carefully and methodically assembled book on Tae Kwon Do: Basics, Techniques and Forms.

MASTER ALLAN SCHEIN

Master Allan Schein is a 5th Dan black belt, small businessman and former endurance athlete living and teaching in Salt Lake City. Having grown up in the Bronx and Yonkers, New York, Master Schein resided in Boston before moving to Vermont as an adult and beginning his training in Tae Kwon Do.

As a long distance athlete, participating in swimming, bicycling, cross country skiing and snowshoeing events, he brought a high fitness and endurance level, as well as exceptional personal discipline, to his Tae Kwon Do training. Allan took naturally to the martial arts

under the personal tutelage of Master Mike Palumbo. Master Palumbo was amongst the earliest students of Grandmaster Park when he moved to Jersey City in 1971. Mike was one of the first student instructors in Grandmaster Park's school, and was given the extraordinary compliment of being showcased with "perfect technique". Mike trained with several of the greats of the day, including Gerard Robbins and Dennis Robinson.

Allan trained in the traditional manner exactly as Grandmaster Park had instructed and taught Mike. Not having a formal training place at his Plainfield home, Mike began teaching a handful of students, including Allan, on the lawn in his backyard. For many of those first years that they trained together, Allan and Mike trained in what they referred to as "berserker style". They trained long, hard hours, day after day, occasionally outdoors, training in the snowy Vermont winters. They cut firewood and moved logs for fun, fuel and fitness. When winter came, they trained in a wood paneled garage in Mike's old barn; a room built for a former owner's prized Packard. Many a heavy bag was ripped from the ceiling over the next few years. For a while, a young drummer had his percussion set up at one end of this garage, and when they worked out, they had rhythm to train by. And a tempo you could barely keep up with. Allan found Tae Kwon Do particularly rewarding; it improved his flexibility, his confidence, his ability to defend himself, and his knowledge and respect for himself and others. It also brought him into contact, and fostered friendships with many other practicing martial artists.

They trained in the garage, in available living rooms, basements, and barns for years, until opportunity presented them with a Dojang space. It was an old dance hall, with hard maple floors and high ceilings, which was generously donated by local businessman Alan Goldman. Mike now had a formal space in which to train and teach. The school was named Green Mountain Martial Arts, and flourished as a small but important Vermont school in the 1980's and 90's. Several years later, the school's location changed to the "Hay Barn" at local Goddard College in Plainfield. And several years after that, Mike rebuilt the barn beside his home to create his own Dojang in the upper half. Allan assisted teaching with Mike at each location, and Allan found it infinitely rewarding to watch students they had taught together grow up from young sprouts to towering trees, and become leaders and fully contributing members of our communities. To this day, Mike and Allan remain the best of friends.

Allan and Mike competed throughout Vermont in local and regional tournaments. Although doing well in all event categories, Allan excelled as a "breaker" and won the gold at numerous events. In addition to bricks, he has demonstrated the ability to break river stones, leaf springs, the necks off bottles, stacks of blocks, tiles, and granite slabs. There is a story about a small mountain of broken bricks and stones in the back yard of Allan's Vermont home. When he put it up for sale, a local realtor brought by a potential buyer who wanted to know what the structural problems were with his house. The buyer had seen piles of broken bricks ten feet from the house, and in his mind, there had to be a connection. The realtor explained about Allan's Tae Kwon Do, but the buyer still did not understand. So the realtor walked up to Allan's office upstairs in his little barn and asked him to demonstrate a brick break. Allan walked to his breaking table (a 15" thick granite block) and broke a brick in half as a matter of routine, tossing the broken pieces onto the pile. The people were a little disbelieving, so Allan broke another brick, and tossed that on the pile as well. And even though they had just witnessed what Allan did, up close and personal, they still wanted to know what the problem was with the house. They never did buy it.

In the mid nineties, Allan moved to Salt Lake City, Utah, where he continued his training and teaching at a local Dojang. Having the need to travel regularly for business and various events, Allan got into the habit of finding a good Tae Kwon Do school in each city he frequented. He also trained in other styles to supplement his knowledge and understanding of each. In recent years, Allan has built a formal Dojang at his Salt Lake home, and teaches in between his travels.

Allan has developed a strong specialty in women's self defense. One evening during his high school years, when walking the dog with his brother, they heard a woman screaming. Upon investigating, they learned two young girls were being attacked behind the local high school just beside their location. One of the girls, who had gotten away, and Allan's brother went for help while Allan went to find the missing victim. He went a short way behind the school building and found two of his high school classmates trying to rape a younger friend. Allan managed to stop their attempt and prevent the rape, but being at a physical disadvantage against two opponents, he was more persuasive then forceful. His own lack of martial ability when he needed it, and the unjust and vicious attack on an innocent teenage friend, strongly influenced his desire to empower women with the ability and skills to properly defend themselves.

He currently resides and teaches in the Salt Lake area.

HISTORY OF TAE KWON DO

Early Tae Kwon Do

The ancestors of the Korean peoples inhabited the Korean peninsula sometime after the Neolithic age. These early inhabitants lived in tribal states, and were strongly influenced by their Chinese and Manchurian neighbors. Northern Korea is a rugged mountainous area with little agricultural land. The local tribes turned to hunting for their food, and further developed their hunting skills into a martial way of life. The Korean peninsula has always been in conflict because it lies at the crossroads of Asia. The Chinese, Japanese and Russians have long sought after its lands. It is alleged that there were 900 different wars in Korea's 5,000-year history. Partly as a result of this, Korean peoples have developed as survivors, and are truly an indomitable people. They are also extremely political, and in this respect have negotiated successfully enough as a nation and fought hard enough in battle to have never been conquered, until the 1910 Japanese occupation. The history and culture of the Korean people has led them to develop a strong spirit of independence and personal growth. As individuals, they are exceptional people, excelling and dis-

tinguishing themselves at most anything they attempt. From 1945, when various Kwans of Tae Kwon Do resurfaced, the growth of Tae Kwon Do has been enormous. Korean Masters went forth in the 1960's to spread this art around the globe. By 2005 there were 179 member nations in the World Taekwondo Federation, with more than 60 million practitioners around the world. It is unlikely that Tae Kwon Do will ever be in danger of becoming a forgotten art again.

Ancient Koreans practiced various sports that, through growing popularity and practice, evolved into an early form of Tae Kwon Do called Taekyon. Eventually, these Taekyon techniques were taught to warriors because of their martial application. The fighting system expanded as martial systems due to their useful military applications. Taekyon and Subaki were early forms of foot fighting that began as sports. Taekyon is the earliest name of Tae Kwon Do. It is the root of Tae Kwon Do and the inspiration for its modern name.

The ancient history of Korea placed its geographical position at the crossroads of Asia. The peninsula served as a bridge between the mainland, Japan, China and more northern areas. In later centuries, when Japan attempted attacks on China, it did so through the Korean mainland.

In the early years of Korean history, there were three separate dynasties or kingdoms, each occupying a different area on the peninsula. Koguryo controlled the north, Silla the southeast, and Paekjae the southwest. These early years were filled with attempts by the Chinese, the Japanese, and other enemies of the Korean people at the time, to try to conquer the peninsula. It was a war filled period and militaristic societies and alliances evolved as a matter of necessity.

Taekyon was popular enough during the **Koguryo Dynasty** (37BCE – 668CE) for murals to be painted in royal tombs, as archeologists discovered in 1935. These images depict men facing each other in poses similar to modern Tae Kwon Do stances. Another depicted two men wrestling in what appears to be the Korean art of Ssirium, further attesting to the popularity of martial arts during this period. The Koguryo dynasty was situated in the north near Manchuria, in Hwando province. In its early days, the kingdom formed a warrior corps called the "Sunbae". The ancient meaning of Sunbae is "a man of virtue who never recoils from a fight". It is reputed that the Sunbae lived in groups, learning history, the arts, and constructing roads and fortresses for the benefit of the kingdom. Eventually Koguryo fell to Silla forces in 668CE, completing the initial unification of the Korean peninsula.

The **Paekjae Kingdom** (18BCE – 600CE) occupied the lands in the southwest of the Korean Peninsula. Paekjae and Silla attempted several times to conquer each other, with Paekjae finally accomplishing this feat in 400CE. But in 661, Silla turned the tides, defeating Paekjae. Then several years later, both Silla and Paekjae were both conquered by Koguryo, fully unifying the peninsula.

The Hwarangdo warriors appeared during the **Silla Dynasty** (57BCE – 935CE) which had its capitol at Kyongju in the south-eastern region of Korea. During the sixth century CE, Bhuddism was first introduced to Silla. This was a period of great nationalism and the culture evolved into a society that emphasized the military and education, and was led by the upper class, or noble youth, of the era. The Hwarangdo warriors lived by a strict code outlined by the Bhuddist monk Won'gwang (531 – 630CE) in the early 600's CE. The code states:

1) Loyalty to one's King
2) Respect and obedience to one's parents
3) Fidelity and good faith in friendship
4) Never to retreat in battle
5) Never to make an unjust kill

This Hwarangdo code has similarities to today's tenets of Tae Kwon Do, and through this common philosophy we are further linked to our Tae Kwon Do past. The Hwarangdo were an elite youth corps, well educated, well practiced in the military arts, and highly organized at the local level. After the three kindgdoms were unified, there followed a relatively peaceful period. During this time, the Hwarang became known more for cultural and artistic pursuits, and gradually declined as a military organization.

Unification under the Silla lasted only about two hundred years, and divided once again into the original three kingdoms. But by the end of the tenth century, unification would become permanent, and the new kingdom was born, which would be known as Koryo.

THE MIDDLE YEARS

The **Koryo Dynasty** (936CE – 1392CE) witnessed Subak becoming popular as a martial art and sport. It thrived during this period, reaching its height of popularity in the mid 12th century. Historical accounts report activity in several provinces where people gathered to compete in Subak. Other accounts make reference to gatherings of people who watch Subak as a spectator sport. Its popularity was at a peak, and corresponded to a similar period in history that saw the development of the Chinese art of Kung Fu. The Shaolin Monks of China had developed their system of Kung Fu by this time, and there is indication that some Koreans were influenced by it.

In the late Koryo era, the Korean people of the time participated in the Mongol conquest and expansion of their empire. These conquests extended far to the west, as far as the Danube River. Koryo territory was also the launching ground for the failed Mongol attack on Japan. This attack from the sea was prevented by heavy storms. The event of nature was so fortunate for the Japanese that they named it "divine wind" or "Kamikaze".

The **Chosun Dynasty,** also known as the **Yi Dynasty** (1392CE – 1910CE) came to power in the 14th century, which saw the decline of the Mongols and growth and influence of the Chinese Ming Dynasty. Yi Songgye came into power, taking the name King Taejo; and in 1392 Confucianism replaced Bhuddism as the state religion. This new philosophy put greater value and emphasis on the arts, poetry, reading, and music. The spiritual was emphasized, and the importance of the physical was reduced. Although martial arts practice continued to grow, it still remained in the shadow of intellectualism. During his reign King Chongjo ordered the publication of an illustrated martial arts book published. The "Muye Dobo Tongji", written by Yi Duk-Moo, included extensive information about Subak including 38 illustrations in the fourth chapter that closely resemble today's Tae Kwon Do moves. The Yi dynasty lasted until 1910 with the formal occupation of Korea by the Japanese. The Japanese removed the then newly reigning king from power, thus ending the Yi dynasty, and the long line of kings that had ruled until Japanese occupation.

THE MODERN YEARS

The Occupation Years 1910 - Aug 15, 1945

In the late 19th century, after a period of war between the Japanese and Chinese, and roughly ten years later between the Japanese and Russians, the Japanese asserted their power on the Korean peninsula. In 1910 they occupied Korea, removed the king from power, and essentially subjugated the Korean people. They banned the Korean language from the press, made the teaching of Japanese compulsory in schools, and in general frowned upon the Korean culture. At the end of World War II, the Americans banded together on Korean soil to push out the Japanese, and get a foothold against the Russians. Freedom came on August 15, 1945, and Korean culture began to reassert itself.

In 1948, Korea was divided in half by the Americans and Russians, yielding The Peoples Republic of Korea in the North, which was under the Russian's control; the South became The Republic of Korea under America's control. Each country claimed the whole of Korea, and war broke out when North Korean troops invaded South Korea in 1950. War ravaged the Korean peninsula for three years. The Korean War lasted until July 27th, 1953, ending with a division of the country into two Koreas.

In 1952, South Korean President Syngman Rhee had seen a demonstration of Tae Kwon Do and, being suitably impressed, declared that learning this art would become a part of military life.

The years after the war were fraught with political change and turbulence. But although this influenced, and still seems to influence Tae Kwon Do, this period witnessed the formal unification and resurrection of Tae Kwon Do. On April 11, 1955, the various Kwans (schools or associations), which had begun to reform after World War II, officially united under the name Tae Soo Do. The prevailing Kwans at the time were Chung Do Kwan, Moo Duk Kwan, Yun Moo Kwan, Chang Moo Kwan, Oh Do Kwan, Jido Kwan, Chi Do Kwan and Song Moo Kwan. In 1957 the name Tae Kwon Do was formally created and assumed, linking directly to its history of Taekyon. It became recognized worldwide within a decade.

In the late 1950's and 1960's, Korean Masters began going abroad and teaching Tae Kwon Do. Jhoon Rhee, often considered the "Father of American Tae Kwon Do", came to attend college in the United States, first settling in Texas, and later moving to the Washington, DC area. The late 1960's and 1970's saw a large influx of Korean Masters emigrating to the USA and elsewhere around the world. In part, political unrest in Korea influenced relocation and opened the door to new opportunities.

On Sept 16, 1961, the KTA (Korea Tae Kwon Do Association) was established by presidential decree with its first president being General Hong Hi Choi. Shortly after that, on Feb 25, 1962, the KTA joined the Korean Amateur Sports Association. Tae Kwon Do was adopted as a Korean medal sport and becomes part of physical education classes throughout the nation. Additionally, General Choi instructed that all Korean military personnel under his command would train in Tae Kwon Do. The Korean National Police and Air Force instituted the same training policy.

On Oct 9, 1963, at the 44th National Athletic Meet, Tae Kwon Do became an official sport for the first time. Through the development of competition rules and equipment instituted at this time, we were given the basis for today's sophisticated competitions.

In 1963, General Choi split off from the KTA as a separate organization and formed the ITF (International Tae Kwon Do Federation). Ultimately, he fell out of political favor in Korea and, in 1972, General Choi relocated his ITF headquarters to Canada where he lived until his death in 2002.

In 1972, the Kukkiwon, also known as The World Taekwondo Headquarters, was established.

On May 28, 1973, the First Tae Kwon Do World Championships were held at Kukkiwon in Seoul.

In 1973, Korea Tae Kwon Do Association became the World Tae Kwon Do Federation (WTF), the governing world organization for Tae Kwon Do, with representatives joining from all 19 participating countries attending these world championships.

In 1980, the World Taekwondo Federation and Kukkiwon officially established headquarters in Seoul, Korea.

In 1988, Tae Kwon Do was an official demonstration sport at the 24th Olympics in Seoul, Korea, and again in 1992 at the 25th Olympics in Barcelona, Spain.

In 2000, Tae Kwon Do became an official sport at the 27th Olympics in Sydney, Australia. Tae Kwon Do teams competed at the 2004 28th Olympic games in Athens, Greece, and it will continue to be a medal sport in 2008 at the 29th Olympic games in Beijing, China, as well as at the 30th Olympic games in London, England, in 2012.

From its ancient beginnings and the martial practices of a warlike tribal society, Tae Kwon Do has evolved into an art and sport recognized and practiced in nearly every nation on Earth. In 60 years, it has progressed from an outlawed practice to an international art and sport that continues to grow in popularity and practice. The early codes that defined the acceptable behavior and dictated the righteous application still live on today through the tenets of Tae Kwon Do, which embody the spirit and essence of the art. Instructors and Masters around the world continue to teach a sense of responsibility and emphasize the important spiritual and personal aspects, as well as foster a higher moral character in students so they understand their responsibility as members of our community and society.

PHILOSOPHY

It is important to remember that Tae Kwon Do is an art—a martial art. And that means there is much more to it than the sports side. Although Tae Kwon Do grew from the need to hunt and defend ourselves and our families, in modern times we need martial skills less and less. However, the art and sport of Tae Kwon Do is widely practiced and accepted because of its many practical benefits. It improves practitioners' physical conditioning, health and flexibility, as well as offering invaluable knowledge on self defense and giving those

involved a supportive community. It requires respect for yourself and others, self discipline, commitment, practice and skill. Tae Kwon Do should only be used for good and peaceful purposes. Never misuse what you have learned, and avoid as best you can any physical confrontation outside of your supervised training. Learn to have power over your actions and your emotions, and do not use Tae Kwon Do in haste or in anger. Set a good example for your training partners and those that follow you into training. Maintain an indomitable spirit, yet remain contemplative and diplomatic in your responses.

Tae Kwon Do is a Korean martial art and its evolution has been guided and heavily influenced by Asian philosophy. The Taegeukki, or Korean National flag, clearly represents this philosophy through the inclusion of the Um-Yang and trigram symbols. Essentially, the eight trigrams (four of which are represented on the flag) represent all that happens in heaven and on Earth. At the same time, the trigrams were held to be in a state of continual transition, one changing into another, just as transitions from one phenomenon to another are continually taking place in the physical world. The trigrams are symbols standing for changing transitional states; they are images that are constantly undergoing change. The focus is not on things in their physical state of being, but upon their movements in change. The Um-Yang (Yin-Yang in Chinese) represents this with the two opposing halves being separated with an S-shaped line, in which it appears that one half flows to the other half. Um-Yang represents the opposites in life, though they struggle together while cooperating in harmony. Positive and negative, light and dark, right and wrong, male and female, black and white, are examples of Um-Yang. Based partly from this influence, the tenets of Tae Kwon Do were created, and these strong principles and codes of behavior survive in principle and in practice to this day.

Over the millennia, a level of escalation was described through the martial arts that urged using only the appropriate level of force necessary to defuse or respond to a confrontation. It goes like this:

Avoid, rather than confront.
Confront, rather than hurt.
Hurt, rather than injure.
Injure, rather than maim.
Maim, rather than kill.
Kill, rather than be killed.

There is no shame in walking away from a confrontation if it keeps you or an aggressor from getting hurt. But things do happen, and should they ever happen to you, keep a calm, clear and focused head on your shoulders. See things for what they are, and respond accordingly. Should you be required to respond to aggression, do what is necessary to defend yourself and other innocent people. Your years of training will prepare you to make a sound decision and respond appropriately to the situation.

As a beginning student, we wish to encourage your training to the fullest extent of your ability. You are beginning to learn an ancient and revered system of accumulated knowledge that is both an art and a lifestyle. It is an art in the sense that there are myriad studied actions and executions for Tae Kwon Do techniques. It is also an art of practiced performance and graceful presentation. In the beginning, you may feel uncoordinated, even clumsy with your training. But with practice, your body will develop reflex memory, and your actions will be automatic, along pre-developed nerve pathways. Your mind and your body both have memory ability, and both will be developed through your training. Depending on your school, you may learn to meditate. Meditation is an excellent tool to carry out of the Dojang and into your daily life. It is a process of calming, clearing and focusing your mind on a given subject. It allows you to concentrate your energy by focusing the mind and clearing out any thoughts unrelated to the subject at hand. Be it in a reflective and introspective way or through direct and rapid focus of attention. Forms, or Poomse, are often practiced as moving meditation.

Discipline is a primary theme in all martial arts training. Some people learn it early in their homes, but all students need to learn and apply discipline to their efforts and behavior in the Dojang. There will be a time in your life when what you learn in school (or in the Dojang) will be taken with you into your daily life. Your self-discipline and your character may be two of the most important things that Tae

Kwon Do will help to nourish and develop. Your physical growth is more obvious day to day, but the person you are, and the character traits you bring to any given situation, are what will make a positive difference in your life. Discipline means working hard, training to learn Tae Kwon Do's rules, techniques and applications, being persistent and regular, developing skill and strength over time, making friends, helping your fellows, and staying the course. There will be days you hurt or just don't feel up to training. It's important to train on as many of those days as possible, because in reality your body may automatically wake up during your warm-ups, even though you are unfocused and your mind is elsewhere. Merely commencing your daily routine often helps to center yourself and bring your focus to the moment and to your training, and it also helps you to forget for a while any poor feelings, or mental distractions. Your training will become a center point in your life, through its regularity, fun atmosphere, sense of camaraderie, healthy workouts, wealth of knowledge and family atmosphere. The discipline will foster greater confidence, self-respect and increased abilities.

THE NATIONAL FLAGS

Every nation on Earth has a national flag that symbolizes the ideals, history and culture of that country. Every day you enter your Dojang, you will bow with respect to your US and the Korean national flag. So it is good to have an understanding of the meanings of each nation's flag.

The **American flag** is also called Old Glory, The Star Spangled Banner, The Stars and Stripes, or The Red, White and Blue. In May 1776, Betsy Ross reported that she had sewn the first American flag. It contained thirteen stripes, representing the original thirteen colonies, and the Union jack in the upper left corner. On June 14, 1777 (June 14 is Flag Day) the Continental Congress passed the first flag act: "Resolved, That the flag of the United States be made of thirteen stripes, alternate red and white; that the union be thirteen stars, white in a blue field, representing a new Constellation." These thirteen stars were arranged in a circle. As our nation grew, and more states became part of America, the flag was redesigned to reflect each new state. The thirteen stripes representing the original colonies remained constant, with new states having their star added to the flag on July 4th of the year that they were admitted to the Union. The 50th star was added on July 4, 1960 to represent the addition of Hawaii as a state.

The colors used in the flag are also symbolic. The red symbolizes hardiness and valor, the white symbolizes innocence and purity, and the blue symbolizes vigilance, perseverance and justice. Overall our flag stands for "Freedom and Justice for All".

The **Korean national flag**, also called the Taegeukki or Taegeukdo, symbolizes the Asian philosophy of existence. It originates from the ancient Asian philosophy of Um-Yang, or as the Chinese call it, the Yin-Yang, which believes the principle that all things have a dual force that governs all existence. A positive and negative side, a light and dark, hard and soft, right and wrong, good and bad, male and female, hot and cold, rich and poor, life and death. Um and Yang are opposite, struggling with each other while they cooperate in harmony. Um's and Yang's harmonious state of movement is called the principle of Palgwe, or Taegeuk. The trigrams (also known as "gwe" signs) symbolize the principle of the movement within all objects in the universe, and the movement of the Universe itself.

The circle in the middle is called the Um-Yang, and is divided by an "S"-shaped line that divides the circle into two interflowing halves, the upper one which is red (Yang), the lower half which is blue (Um). The four trigrams in the corners of the flag are divination symbols, and represent the four elements, four directions of the compass, and the four seasons. The broken bars symbolize "Um", and the solid bars "Yang". The trigrams are placed opposite in such a way that they balance each other. Heaven is placed opposite of earth; fire is placed opposite of water. There are eight trigrams in total, only four of which appear on the national flag. All 8 trigrams and their meanings are further described in the chapter on forms, which is entitled Poomse.

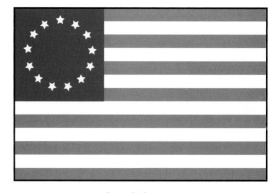

The American Flag, Old Glory

The upper left trigram, Keon Gwe, represents air, heaven, and the South. It also signifies "Full Light, or Day".

The opposite trigram in the lower right, Kon Gwe, stands for the earth, and the North. It also signifies "Total Darkness".

The upper right trigram, Kam Gwe, represents water and the West. It also signifies twilight, and the setting sun.

The opposite lower left trigram, Ri Gwe, represents fire, and the East. It also means "Dawn and the Rising Sun".

The white background represents the peace and purity of the Korean peoples.

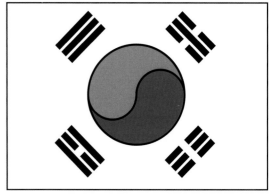

Korean National Flag, The Taegeukdo

Your instructors, Master (Sabum nim) and Grandmaster (Kwan jang nim) are your teachers, guides, best examples and inspiration in learning Tae Kwon Do. All have trained in a similar manner to how you will be taught, and they have trained for many years. If you travel around the world you will find that the Tae Kwon Do you practice in America is basically the same as that in Korea, Europe, Africa, and Asia. It is not unusual for Grandmasters to train and teach for 50 years before reaching Tae Kwon Do's highest belt rank of 9th Dan (degree), having started as a young person. Officially, there is no rank higher than 9th degree black belt in Tae Kwon Do. By today's criteria, the rank of Grandmaster in the USA can be attained at 7th Dan, and Master at 4th Dan. Black belts are registered through the Kukkiwon or official Korean Entity for registering World Taekwondo Federation (WTF) belt holders. In America, only black belt ranks are registered through the Kukkiwon. Lower rank belts, also known as colored belts, are periodically awarded at local school testings by the officiating Master or Grandmaster.

Belts progress from white belt, to 9th Gup (grade), or yellow belt, and on up in rank to 8th Gup, 7th, all the way to 1st Gup, usually signified as a red or brown belt. Belt color systems will vary between different schools. Usual progression is yellow, orange, green, blue, purple, brown and red, with some having high and low red or blue belts. Gup levels are the same in all schools, and techniques and Poomse (forms) for each level are similar as well.

It is usual for pictures of the Grandmaster and all the schools' Masters to be placed prominently in the school. This familiarizes the students with all the school's Master instructors, and appropriately acknowledges the Masters themselves.

CHOOSING A SCHOOL (DOJANG)

To choose the correct school, you need to make sure that you know what you want from Tae Kwon Do. If you want to train to be a champion, find a school with a history of successful competitors. If you want to be a good martial artist, and since this is not always the same as the school that wins the most championships, your search should consider that as well. First, locate the schools in your area and take some time to visit them. Have a discussion with the schoolmaster. You will probably be invited to join or watch classes to get a feel for them. Speak with other students and parents and get their impressions of the school and Master. A good Master will lead by example, and as you must be worthy of becoming his or her student, so must the Master be worthy of the student. See these Masters as the people they are, not who you want them to be. Most Masters are caring, understanding community leaders. But a few rely upon dubious credentials and some even make up histories to suit their situations. You should get a sense of the instructors and the students because they are a direct reflection of the school Master.

THE DOJANG

After an introduction with your Tae Kwon Do Master or Grandmaster, you will probably take a white belt or beginner class to see how you like it. Should you discover you like it, start regular classes. Once you start you will find your school or "Dojang" to look like most other Dojangs: there will be a large open room with padded, carpeted or wooden floors. You will have purchased a training uniform or Dobok, which should always be clean when attending class. Approach the room or training floor at attention. Bow towards the national flags to show respect, and bow to your Masters and Grandmaster. Enter onto the floor and line up according to belt order, new beginners with no belts or white belts being in the last position. Conversely, the highest and most senior belt wearer stands in the first position. This is in the front row, all the way to the right, facing the national flags. You will not wear shoes (unless martial art training shoes with approval) or bring food into the Dojang. Classes will begin with a "bowing in". When class is led by a Grandmaster, often the students as well as Grandmaster will kneel and touch their heads to the ground in a formal mutual bow of respect. The traditional bow is from attention stance, bending at the waist 15-20° with the head bent at 45°. Eyes are looking at the ground. (Please note that when bowing before sparring, your eyes will face your opponent.) A series of warm-up exercises will be performed which include stretching, kicking and punching exercises, calisthenics, sit-ups, and running, etc. All classes will include at least some of these, and often vary their routines every day adding variety. Old school masters tend to keep to regular routines so all students get to know them, and teach them when given the opportunity. Your assistant instructors, (usually new black belts and instructors ranking in belt up to 3rd Dan) all started by leading warm-ups at some point in their intermediate or higher training.

There is a set of Dojang rules that must be obeyed by all students at the school. All schools ask that you learn these and agree to them. Most schools have a school code and rules posted visibly for everyone to see and as a reminder that we train as a team and family, and are of one discipline.

The typical school code follows:

1) Respect each other.
2) Always stand by the weak.
3) Be loyal to yourself, your Dojang, and your community.
4) Obey and be loyal to your Sabum nim (Master instructor).

The typical school rules are as follows:

1) When you enter the Dojang, bow to national flags, Sabum nim, and fellow students.
2) When you leave the Dojang, bow to students, flags, and Sabum nim.
3) Whenever you arrive during a class already in session, enter the Dojang and wait on one knee for your Sabum nim's, or the class instructor's permission to enter.
3) The following are prohibited in the Dojang: street shoes, smoking, intoxication, chewing gum, loud laughter, bad language, arguing, food.
4) Always wear a clean Dobok to class with school patch. Avoid wearing jewelry.
5) Whenever you approach your Sabum nim, bow first and then speak to him politely.
6) Whenever you need assistance simply inform your Sabum nim that you do not know a particular movement and trust he will take care of you.
7) All students must be courteous and obey their Sabum nim. Advanced students should set a good example for lower belts.
8) Do not demonstrate or teach Tae Kwon Do outside the Dojang without permission of your Sabum nim. Never degrade Tae Kwon Do or the reputation of your school.
9) You must have permission from your Sabum nim to participate in any tournament or martial art activity. Awards shall be displayed at school.

Our lineage is from one of the old Kwans of Tae Kwon Do. Jido Kwan can literally be translated as the "Way of Wisdom" and is referred to as the "House of Discipline". The teachings and rules of Jido Kwan follow the "Spirit of the Eight Fold Path". These are:

1) View Rightly
2) Fell Rightly
3) Think Rightly
4) Speak Rightly
5) Order Rightly
6) Contribute Rightly
7) Have Ability
8) Conduct Rightly

Tae Kwon Do training is seriously interested in making sure those that learn the Art do not misuse their ability. The eight-fold path is a series of commandments by which the ideal martial artist will live. In this manner Tae Kwon Do can be used for peaceful, instead of warlike, purposes. You are making an agreement with your Sabum nim, if he is willing to take you on as a student. You agree not to abuse the knowledge he shares and will not "demonstrate" and possibly injure another person. You will be wise in your use of what you are taught.

Your uniform or **Dobok** is designed for Tae Kwon Do training. It consists of a loose fitting top jacket called the "Uht-doree", loose fitting pants called "Ba-jie" and a belt called a "Thee". The color of your belt depends upon your achieved rank, and will change as you progress. All Tae Kwon Do practitioners wear a white Dobok but may have distinguishing markings, especially Grandmasters. Black belts wear a Dobok with black trim around the V-neck of their uniform. Most schools have their own embroidered patch for identification, uniformity and pride. Some patches incorporate signs and symbols of their original Kwans or schools. You will see fists, kicking profiles and the like. All are distinctive. Additionally, many schools require a patch for the member organization, such as the World Taekwondo Federation (WTF), or an American and/or Korean national flag.

Belt ranks are levels achieved after considerable practice and demonstration of ability. The belt system is a symbol measuring the progression of a student's ability and accomplishments in Tae Kwon Do. Beginners start as white belts. Levels progress upwards with the learning of various kicking and punching techniques, self defense techniques and fighting patterns (Poomse). With each level comes another belt attained, from 9th Gup up to 1st Gup, or high red belt or brown belt.

Belt color progression varies a bit from school to school. At the main DK Park school, the belt color system is as follows: white, yellow, high yellow, green, high green, blue, high blue, red and high red. To make up for the different number of Gups over colors, schools have low and high belts, orange and brown belts as needed. Gup levels are basically the same as far as level of accomplishment, or relatively equal, from school to school. There are also various accomplishment levels recognized between belt tests, earning the student a yellow belt with black stripe, for example. Belt stripes are most common where younger children practice and make up a majority of the student body. They are awarded by instructors and Masters when students demonstrate their knowledge of a new set of testing requirements.

At black belt, you have grown beyond the Gup level, and now we count upwards in degrees. Black belts are required to wait a minimum of six months before attaining Dan ranking. This waiting period is known as probabtion, and these black belts are known as deputy black belts, probation black belts, or recommended black belts. The probation black belt is often two tones, with the upper half black, and lower half red. Each will need to test again to reach full Dan or first degree black belt ranking. Please note that young students are given "Poom" ranking that automatically converts to Dan ranking at the age of 15. Ranking moves upward thereafter based upon ability, contribution to Tae Kwon Do, and active time training. Modern ranking in the USA requires a minimum of:

> 1 to 2 years to go from 1st Dan to 2nd Dan
> 2 to 3 years to go from 2nd Dan to 3rd Dan
> 3 to 4 years to go from 3rd Dan to 4th Dan
> and on like that.

A 4th Dan is considered a Master in the USA. A 7th Dan and above is considered a Grandmaster. 9th Degree black belt is the highest official rank in Tae Kwon Do.

TESTING

Students will be tested periodically by their Masters and Grandmasters to determine their level of ability. This allows them to demonstrate their knowledge of the techniques and patterns of Tae Kwon Do. Even beginners must show they try hard and deserve to become white belts by learning a few basic kicks and punches before putting on a white belt. From the day you start training, you will be taught the basic kicks and punches, blocks and strikes, stances and movements, self defense moves and fighting patterns (or forms, called Poomse) that are the foundation for sparring techniques and self defense. Each belt level has a different set of combination kicking techniques getting progressively more complex and difficult, from a basic stepping front kick to

Examples of Dobok patches used by schools

a stepping jump spinning hook kick. You will see the progression of your growing ability, and be asked to show proficiency in all things taught to you.

A typical test consists of a panel of Masters and Grandmasters gathered together to judge the ability of each student individually, though much of your testing may be done with other fellow belt holders. There will be a formal bow-in, introductions, and testing will then start with the lowest belt rank, white belts testing for yellow belt. Students will demonstrate their basic combination kicking and punching techniques, their Poomse, self defense techniques, breaking technique and answer questions as asked by the judging panel. If a student makes a mistake, they are given a chance to correct it. Students that pass their tests receive a certificate of rank, much like a diploma, and their next belt. As testing progresses from rank to rank, there are additional requirements, such as sparring, special techniques, breaking and general knowledge. During testing, you may be called upon to show or demonstrate anything you have been taught since you began training (including, but not limited to, techniques, rules, formalities, principles and history).

Your first class will begin like every class, with students lining up according to belt rank, with the highest belt in a class (usually a black belt in advanced classes) standing in what is called the first position, in the first row at the front of the class, all the way to the right. Students with the next highest belt ranks will line up to the left of the first position, and on back into the next rows.

STRETCHING (pyoogi) may be the single most important activity you can perform for your body. Did you ever watch a dog or cat when they first awaken from a nap or sleep? They stretch. It's a slow but deliberate body length elongation of their entire frame. And then they get up and proceed on towards their intended activity, whatever that might be. Tae Kwon Do teaches stretching as a total body routine, designed to prevent injuries, prepare you for Tae Kwon Do exercises, and maximize your flexibility. You will be amazed at the difference in your flexibility in as little as two weeks. Everyone can increase their flexibility simply by being regular with a routine, and moderately working at it. You will feel better, and that is only one of the many benefits.

After the formal bow-in, class will commence with head to toe stretches of your neck, shoulders, arms, wrists and hands, torso, back, hips, knees, legs, and feet. Of the two primary types of stretches, a static or "stretch and hold" technique is most effective. It allows for a complete and thorough stretch you can relax into and feel, as opposed to ballistic stretching, a more rapid almost callisthenic style.

Warm-ups are equally as important, allowing your muscles to acclimate to the activities soon to be demanded of your body, and ready you for full activity. Warm-ups help avoid unnecessary stress to the muscles, tendons, ligaments, joints and possible injury. Blood and oxygen flow to the body areas as they are worked, and your finely toned and tuned human machine is ready to go to work. Your joints begin to secrete and spread a sinovial fluid, your bodies' natural joint lubrication. This protects your joints from excess wear much the same way as having oil in your car's engine.

Warm-ups will vary slightly by school, but will include at least a few of the following: running around the Dojang, 5 to 10 times around the training floor in each direction. Stomach work like sit-ups and crunches, pushups, jumping jacks and various other calisthenics may follow. Kicking and punching exercises and combinations follow and will usually include 10 kicks with each leg for each kick during the exercise. It is not unusual for a student to perform hundreds of kicks during a single session. At this stage of your class, you may get a brief break, but after this is when the real learning will begin.

After the warm-ups, the class performs a series of **basic techniques.** These would include combinations of kicks, punches and blocks moving backwards and forwards, front and rear, to the side, and increasing in complexity as you get sharper and into the groove of the exercise. At this time, lower belts not yet schooled properly in advanced techniques may be given a break. Assistant instructors will work with these students to keep them from sitting idle, and practice their individual combination techniques, Poomse, or assist with any weaknesses the student might have. For example, this could be a particular kick, combination, self-defense technique, or whatever the student might need coaching with. After advanced techniques, the class will work on practicing different things on different days. These will include one-step self defense techniques, patterns, practical self-defense, forms, sparring techniques, and full on sparring.

After class, there is often a warm down period to allow the body to cool off and perhaps some more time for light stretching. It is at this time that meditation sessions are often incorporated. At the end of class, students will again line up and bow out to the national flags, the instructor or Master and then to each other in formal fashion. Class is then dismissed.

STRETCHING

Stretching exercises vary from school to school, and sometimes from instructor to instructor. The following stretching exercises may be more extensive than you have time for in class, and there are many others that can be done, time allowing. But this will be a good reference guide as to what is possible, and what you may wish to practice both inside and outside the classroom.

Standing stretches

Neck

Standing in natural stance, tilt your head up and to the rear, then down to the front, and repeat. (Fig. 001)

Turn your head fully to the left and to the right, as far as comfortably possible. (Fig. 002)

With face to the front, tilt your head to the shoulder from side to side. (Fig. 003)

Next, circle your head, clockwise and counter-clockwise. (Fig. 004)

Next, shake out your head gently to feel loose.

Shoulders

Standing in natural stance, bring your shoulder up and then to the front, down and then to the rear, performing shoulder rolls, first forwards and then backwards. (Fig. 005)

Next, execute shoulder rolls (or shrugs) and add your entire arms, widening the motion gradually into double arm circles, forwards and backwards. (Fig. 006)

Reach your right hand over and behind your head. Grab your left elbow with your right hand, and pull across, stretching the back of your left arm. Switch sides and repeat. (Fig. 007)

Reach your left arm across the front of your chest and to the right. Take your right arm, and reach under your left elbow, bending the right arm upwards, while pulling your left arm tightly to your chest. This stretches the left shoulder and arm. (Fig. 008)

Swing your right arm in a circle, moving from front to back with an overhead swinging motion, and making large sweeping circles. Reverse directions, and then repeat with your other arm. (Fig. 009)

Using both arms, move them horizontally (parallel to the floor), swinging them first together, touching your opposite shoulder with each. Then in non-stop motion, swing them to the rear, clapping them behind your back. (Fig. 010, 011)

Hands

Open both hands individually as wide as possible, and close tightly and repeat. (Fig. 012)

Massage thumb muscle of the left hand with the four fingers of your right hand. Thumbs lie alongside each other while massaging the big muscle. (Fig. 013)

Place the left thumb over the right thumb knuckle. Place the four fingers on the outside over the knife edge of your hand, putting one hand inside the other, folding your hand in half, thumb-to-pinky, and stretching the back of the hand. (Fig. 014)

Fingers

With your left hand, individually bend each finger of your right hand as far back as is comfortably possible, stretching your finger muscles and tendons. Stretch each finger separately, and then switch hands. (Fig. 015)

Wrists

With your hands in fists, circle your hands to stretch the wrists in both directions. (Fig. 016)

With your right hand flat and open with palm up, grab the fingertips of the other, and bend backwards. Switch hands and repeat. (Fig. 017)

Next, place palm of left hand over the top and knuckles of the right hand, and bend fingers forward, stretching the muscles and tendons on the back of your hand. Switch and repeat. (Fig. 018)

With your left hand, reach under and behind your right hand, placing the four fingers around and over the right hand, grabbing the large muscle of the thumb. Palm is across back of hand, and your left thumb is behind the knife-edge (outer edge) of the left hand. (Fig. 019)

Twist your right hand to the left, pulling with your right hand and stretching the right wrist. (Fig. 020)

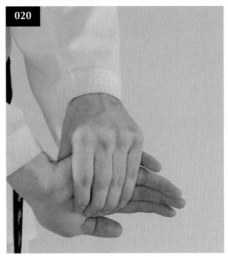

Waist

From natural standing position, place hands on hips, and turn your hips in wide circles, first in one direction, and then the other. (Fig. 021)

From standing natural position, raise your arms, with your elbows at shoulder level and arms bent and at chest level. Turn your upper body all the way to the right and rear, and then to the left and rear. (Fig. 022)

From natural standing position, raise both hands so that they are level in front of you. (Fig. 023) Step right foot back and turn entire body 180° to the rear. (Fig. 024) Return to front and repeat. Perform exercise to both sides.

Reach the left hand overhead, placing the right hand on your waist, and bend deeply to the side while pointing your body and face to the front. Perform to both sides. (Fig. 025)

Bend at your waist, touching both hands to the floor between your feet, and then reach both hands through your legs and behind your feet. Stand up with hands on your waist and lean far back. Repeat. Breathe in on the up motion, and out on the bending motion. (Fig. 026, 027)

Extend both arms out to the side horizontally. Bend to the floor, touching your left hand to your right foot. Your other hand should come up and back. Alternate hands and sides. (Fig. 028, 029)

With both hands extended overhead together, swing your upper body and hands in a circular motion down to the sides, across your front at floor level with fingers sweeping the floor, and up and over on the opposite side. Perform this stretch to both directions. (Fig. 030, 031, 032)

Knees

With feet nearly touching, bend with hands on knees, and circle knees eight to ten times in both directions. (Fig. 033, 034)

Next, with hands on waist and feet slightly apart, perform knee bends, down and up. (Fig. 035)

Legs

Standing on your left leg, bend your right leg to the rear, grasp your foot with the right hand, pull up and behind your body and stretch your hip and thigh muscles. Switch sides and repeat. (Fig. 036)

With a partner in low horse riding stance, extend and raise one leg to the front, placing it on your partner's shoulder. The partner gradually rises into a higher stance until you reach your limit. Switch legs and repeat. Then switch partners. (Fig. 037)

Step your left leg far back and lean forward, keeping the heel of left foot pressed towards the ground, stretching your calf muscle. For a more extreme stretch, lean against a wall and step further back. Switch legs and repeat. (Fig. 038)

From natural stance, take a half step with your right leg to the right. Lean your torso over the extended leg, keeping your leg straight and the knee in a locked position. Bend forward to stretch the back of your thigh. Repeat to both directions. (Fig. 039)

Take a long step to the front with your right leg. Lean forward and stretch your hip. (Fig. 040) From this position, drop your right elbow to your foot on the inside of your leg. (Fig. 041) Drop your weight and stretch your buttock and hip. From this position, turn to your left, and drop your weight so the inside of your left leg feels the stretch. (Fig. 042) Next, twist more to the left, so you now face your left foot, with your left heel on the ground and toes facing up, and drop your weight while leaning to your left foot, stretching your left hamstring (back of the thigh). Switch sides and repeat. (Fig. 043)

Stretches while lying on your back

Lying flat, pull each leg individually to your chest and hold for several seconds. (Fig. 044)

Bend each of your legs individually up and over your torso and across the body, touching your knee to the ground on your opposite side. (Fig. 045)

Take turns placing each leg, which should be fully extended, across your body with your foot at face level or as high as possible. (Fig. 046)

Raise one knee, while keeping the foot flat on the ground. Place the foot of your other leg across your raised knee. (Fig. 047) Reach both hands around raised knee and pull both legs towards your chest, stretching your buttock and lower back. Switch legs and repeat. (Fig. 048)

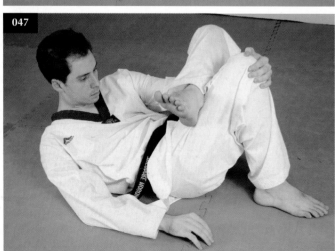

Lying flat, place hands beside hips for back support and move legs in a circle, moving them up, out, and down (but not to the ground). Repeat, and switch directions. (Fig. 049)

Lying flat, rotate your legs as if you were riding a bicycle. Bicycle your legs forward, and then reverse directions. (Fig. 050)

Lying flat, raise both legs fully up and back over your head, let out your breath and touch your feet to the ground above your head. (Fig. 051)

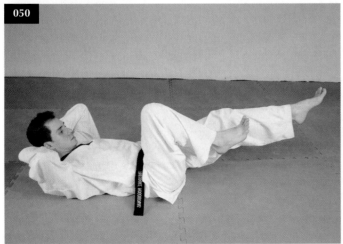

Stretches sitting on ground

Sitting upright, place your right foot over your left knee. Grab the toes of your right foot with your left hand while supporting your right ankle with your right hand, and circle the entire foot widely in both directions. (Fig. 052)

While in the same position, support your heel with one hand while bending the toes and instep all the way forward, stretching the top of the foot. Then pull your toes and foot all the way back, which will stretch the ligaments and muscles of the bottom of your foot. (Fig. 053, 054)

From the same position, twist the blade (outer edge) of the foot towards the floor, stretching the outside of your ankle. (Fig. 055)

From the same leg position, press your right knee down to touch the ground. (Fig. 056)

From the same leg position, reach left arm all the way around your right knee and hook it in the bend of your elbow, pulling the leg to your chest. (Fig. 057)

While the knee is near your chest, place your left arm over the right knee and turn your torso and head to the rear. (Fig. 058)

Complete all stretches to the one side, then switch sides and repeat with other foot and leg.

Sit upright, with your right leg bent, foot pulled towards crotch and your left leg extended straight out. Take a deep breath, turning head away from foot. (Fig.059) Let out breath as you reach both hands forward to touch your left foot. Hold for several seconds, sit up, look rearward, and breath in deeply again. (Fig. 060) Repeat several times. Then switch sides and repeat.

Sitting upright, spread both legs into the split position, with your legs as far to the sides as possible. (Fig. 061)

Raise the level of both arms, elbows bent, and twist and look to the rear, alternating from side to side. (Fig. 062)

Next, place both hands behind your head, and bend side to side, touching your elbows to the ground behind your knee, while keeping your body facing front. Try not to lean forward when performing this exercise. (Fig. 063)

Breathe in deeply and stretch your split a little wider. With both hands, reach and touch the right foot, letting out your breath. Sit up and breathe again, and reach to the left leg. Repeat several times to each side. Make sure both hands touch each foot at the same time. (Fig. 064)

In split position, stretch a bit wider, breath in deeply, and bend forward at the waist, letting out breath. Reach your hands out in front, and touch your chest to the floor if possible. Hold for several seconds, sit up and breathe in, and repeat. Stretch a little wider, and repeat, reaching as far to the front as possible. (Fig. 065)

061

062

063

064

065

Complete this exercise group, return your legs to the front in a relaxed position, and shake it out.

Next, sit upright with both legs straight out in front. Breathe in fully, and bend forward at the waist as you let out your breath. Touch both hands to both feet and hold several seconds. Sit up and repeat. (Fig. 066)

Next, from this position, place the right foot over the top of the left knee and repeat the stretch, touching both hands to the outstretched foot. Switch sides, and repeat. (Fig. 067)

Sit upright, tuck both feet to your crotch, with knees pointing out, in the butterfly position. (Fig. 068) Sit up straight, breath in deeply, and bend at waist to the floor, exhaling as you lean forward. (Fig. 069)

Hold for several seconds, sit up and breathe. Repeat several times.

Sit upright in butterfly position. Place the left hand on the left foot, and your right hand on the left knee by reaching under your left arm. (Fig. 070) Extend your left leg and stretch as you exhale. Pull the leg back to the center, breathing in, and repeat. (Fig. 071) Switch sides and repeat.

In butterfly position, place both hands on both feet (Fig.. 072) and with careful balance, extend both legs fully, remaining upright on your buttocks. (Fig. 073)

Return to a standing position, and shake it out with light jumping to loosen your body.

Stretches on one leg

Stand upright, and drop 100% of your weight onto your right leg while raising the left leg. Grab over the knee with both hands and, with careful balance, pull the left leg to your chest, and hold. (Fig. 074)

From this position, grab your left shin with the left hand, and pull leg into a position level with the floor, twisting your waist slightly to the right. (Fig. 075)

From this position, move your left hand to the front of your lower leg just below the knee, and pull it up as high as possible into a roundhouse position. Return leg to the floor, and repeat to the other side. (Fig. 076)

Stand upright, dropping 100% of your weight to left leg while keeping good balance, raise the right leg, and make circles with the knee from outside to inside, without placing foot to the floor. (Fig. 077)

From this same position, reverse the circular motion with inside to outside circles.

Next, from this position, keeping the knee up in front of you, twist your leg so that your foot swings widely from side to side, loosening your hip joint. (Fig. 078, 079)

Next, balancing extremely well on your bent right leg, grab your left foot with the left hand, (Fig. 080) and fully extend your left leg as high as possible, remaining balanced on the right leg. Switch sides and repeat. (Fig 081)

Extras

From a standing position, drop into a split position, lowering your body as far as possible. (Fig. 082)

From this split position, rotate your body 90° to the right, and perform a front to back split. From this position, rotate your hips 180° in the opposite direction so your other leg extends out front, and stretch as far as possible into a front to back split. (Fig. 083)

Bend down and place your shins flat to the ground in a kneeling position, with toes straight and instep flat. Let your feet relax and flatten to the ground under your weight. (Fig. 084)

From this position, extend arms far to the front, placing one hand on top of the other. Drop head low and press torso to the rear, stretching your shoulders. Alternate which hand is on top and press slightly more with that shoulder. (Fig. 085)

From kneeling position, bend forward, placing the palms of your hands flat in front at shoulder distance. Turn both hands 180° to the inside so your forearms face to the front, fingers pointing to the rear. Keeping your hands flat to the floor, lean back gently and feel your inner forearms stretch. (Fig. 086)

From kneeling position, place the back of your hand flat on the ground with your fingers to the rear. Lean to the rear and stretch the front of your forearms. (Fig. 087)

From this kneeling position, lean fully to the rear, lying flat with head touching the ground, further stretching your stomach, hips and thighs. (Fig. 088)

When stretching is complete, the class will move on to kicking exercises.

STANCES

There are a number of regularly used stances (Seogi) or positions (Jhase) in Tae Kwon Do. Each places the legs and body in a slightly different way, or "stance", allowing for different offensive and defensive movements. They range from the very low and powerful "horse riding stance" to the modern upright and faster "walking stance". Martial arts science tells us that power comes from the ground up. Since we are upright beings, we stand on our feet on this Earth. Pressing up from the Earth gives us solid ground to maneuver from, and this "grounding" gives us tremendous power potential. The lower the stance, the lower our center of gravity and the greater the power we can generate. Conversely, the upright stances, possess much less power, but are more maneuverable and allow greater speed. Lower stances equal power. Upright stances equal speed. In all stances, it is important to maintain a "tight" stomach. This allows us to react quicker by releasing the coiled tension of our muscles.

Most exercises and activities in the Dojang start from the position of **attention** (Char-eot). It is the same stance at attention that the military all over the world uses. You stand straight and tall, heels touching, but the feet turned away slightly at an angle from the center, and your hands flat at your sides. (Fig. 089)

089

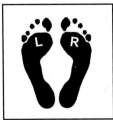

The **ready stance** (Jhoom-be) is a preparatory stance for any subsequent activity. From attention, both hands will be made into fists. Take a deep breath, raise your hands in fists to your chin, and then take a half step out to your left (to one shoulder width apart) while keeping both legs straight. (Fig. 090) Then, and with concentrated power, press your fists down to your center with force and let out your breath. Your fists should stop one fist distance out from your waist, one fist apart from each other and approximately level with your navel. Your arms are parallel and your elbows are slightly out from your body. (Fig. 091) You have now centered yourself, assumed a defensive stance, and are ready for action. Most subsequent stances will start from this position. Your body should remain relaxed and ready for activity. Look straight ahead and be ready!

Our next stance is the **horse riding stance** (Ju choom-jhase). From the ready stance, we step the left foot to the left, wider than the ready stance, to two shoulder widths. Tighten your buttocks and keep your back straight as you lower your center of gravity. Keep your feet pointed straight ahead. At the same time, your arms will prepare for defense, possibly punching or blocking. Start by stepping out to your left, and executing a left hand middle punch. (Fig. 092) This stance is very much the position you would be in if you sat on a horse, but your feet will be directly under your bent legs. Try imagining that you are being held up by a string attached to the center of your head, while keeping your back straight and spring in your legs. You are dangling and supporting yourself on flexible legs. Drop lower into the stance and feel the balance point.

You move in horse riding stance from side to side, or by stepping out at an angle. You can step fully across and end up facing 180° in the opposite direction, while punching or blocking towards the sideways line of movement. Or to remain facing the same direction, step across in front of your left foot with your right foot, thereby not changing the direction of your body. Next, step the left foot sideways all the while staying low and in horse riding position. Turning in horse riding stance requires you first to lift your knee and leg in the direction of motion so that you can powerfully step into the move and execute a strike or block.

092

Horse riding stance also allows for multi-directional strikes and punches. Students usually practice punching to the front in horse riding stance. But you may punch to either side, move from side to side, step across to the opposite side and, from a single position, throw punches to three directions at once all in the same flurry. (Fig. 093, 094, 095, 096, 097)

Front stance (Ap goobe jhase), or forward leaning stance, starts from ready stance (Jhoom-Bee). Take one step to the rear with your right foot, keeping your body facing forward. You could usually add a punch or block, but for now, lets just focus on body position. To enter front stance, you step your right foot straight back, so that you keep the distance between your feet roughly one shoulder width apart. However, you will take a longer step back (two shoulder width), placing the heel of the rear foot solidly on the ground, with your foot turned out to the right at a 45° angle. (Fig. 098) The shin of your front leg should be vertical with your knee just blocking the view of your toes. Keep your back straight and your shoulders turned squarely towards the front. Tense your rear leg so that it is tightly set, pushing forward off your heel. At the same time, press back slightly with the front leg, creating a powerful tension in your hips and legs. (Fig. 099) This tension, or dynamic tension, is what will allow you to spring forward or rearward rapidly and with power when attacking or defending. In Tae Kwon Do, speed and power go hand in hand with every move you execute. We step our right foot back to start an exercise for a very practical reason—it maintains our distance from whoever is in front of us. Should they attack, we are ready. But if we readied ourselves, and took a step forward, it would close the distance between our enemy and immediately place us into the combat zone. There are times when we will want to attack like this, but that will be introduced to you later in combination attacks.

098

099

When moving in the front stance, you need to keep complete balance throughout the movement. First, turn your front (left) foot outward 45° and press the heel to the ground. Bring your rear (right) foot forward, barely skimming the surface of the ground in a generally straight forward movement to the center line, placing it firmly in the forward position. In addition to demonstrating the front stance in the following sequence of movements, Grandmaster simultaneously executes a down block. Further description of this technique will be given in the chapter on blocks. (Fig. 100, 101, 102, 103, 104)

Moving backward is just the reverse. Pull your front foot rearward and complete the rear motion until your foot is set at 45° and a shoulders width apart from your front foot. A common mistake of beginners

is that they tend to "fence-post", or lose the distance between their feet, ending with one foot in a direct line behind the other. If you don't keep the width between them, you have no side-to-side balance, and therefore it becomes a weak stance. There will be no power or control in a stance if there is no balance.

Front stance is not limited in direction, and can move at angles front and back as well as in straight lines. Practice moving at 45° angles, 90° turns to the sides, and complete 180° turns. Once we move on to practicing fighting forms (Poomse) you will learn that we also make 270° turns. Practice front stance to all directions, and if mirrors are available, learn to correct your own body position errors (if you have any). Strive for perfect form.

Turning in front stance requires proper foot adjustments to maintain a solid stance. If your right foot is in front, look over your left shoulder to the rear, and slide your left foot across in front of you (in the direction you are looking) to proper shoulder width spacing as you turn 180°, and then twist your feet and waist, and lean forward into the stance, tensing your legs as earlier described, and keeping your back straight and shoulders square to the front. Turning again to the rear, you would look over your right shoulder, turn 180°, slide your right leg and foot across your front, and again shift hip and leg positions. Please note that this will move your position sideways (crabbing) across a room if you make enough turns. If you're not crabbing sideways during this exercise, your width spacing is probably not correct. Make adjustments as necessary. (Fig. 105, 106, 107, 108)

Back stance (Dwit goobe jhase), is also known as the "L" stance, which describes the position of your feet when it is properly executed. Place your feet together at a 90° angle to each other with the heels touching. Next, bend your right leg and drop your center of gravity onto it, bearing 60% to 80% of your body's weight on this leg. Keep your back straight the entire time. Relax into the stance. Next, slide your left leg in the direction it is pointing, extending the length of the letter "L" pattern made by your feet. The leg should extend apart between one and a half to two times your shoulder width. Your heels should be aligned in a straight line. (Fig. 109) Do not place much weight on the front leg but keep it set for balance. Your upper body is facing the direction that your weighted foot (right) faces, with your left shoulder facing towards your left foot. This is a sideways stance, and you will look forward and to your left, where your opponent stands. Your leg will immediately feel how your weight is balanced. When working on forms, you will want a longer stance of two shoulder widths apart, balanced with 60% of your weight on the rear leg, and 40% on the front. In the longer stance the balance will be awkward with 80% weight to the rear. For fighting, the shorter stance, one and a half shoulder widths with 80% weight to the rear leg is faster and considered the "modern" stance. In this position, you will probably find yourself trying to shift weight to the front foot. Don't do it. Drop your weight lower onto your rear leg, keeping the left foot flat, but only lightly touching the ground. Keep both knees bent.

Here is one of the major advantages of doing this: In some styles, weight is balanced 50-50. But then it becomes a different stance, more like a wide angle horse stance. You can move and fight from there - you will have great balance - but the purpose is different. A true Tae Kwon Do back stance allows you to kick without shifting or moving to another position. Your weight is already on the rear leg, allowing the front to lift immediately without you having to shift your balance. It allows for an immediate counter or attack. Should you first have to shift your weight to the rear foot before you can lift the front foot, you give the advantage away to your opponent. Never give away a martial advantage. You are a martial artist, and as such you will need to learn how to keep, create and maintain an advantage every chance you can. In reality, there are several ways to set your body weight for a back stance, each for a slightly different purpose.

Moving in back stance is in a straight line forward, backward or angular. It requires balance and smooth movements. From the back stance, the stance we are presently standing in, right foot back, you will first turn your left foot 90° to the left. Next, lean into your left foot and begin to transfer your weight to the left leg. As you are doing this, you will "step" your right foot over your left foot, while dropping your weight onto the left leg. Move your right foot in a straight line forward. Your body will make the 180° turn automatically in the process. Extend your right foot forward, setting it with light weight on it for proper balance. (Fig. 110, 111)

Turning is very simple in back stance. (Fig. 112, 113, 114) With your right foot forward, simply twist your feet 90° to the left on both heels. Both heels stay down. Drop your weight onto the right leg, which is now your rear leg. By moving your feet 90° to one side or the other, and shifting your weight, you can face two directions rapidly with only a slight turn of the body. This is a practical stance and uses economy of motion.

Walking stance (Ap seogi jhase), or natural stance, is an upright stance using your normal stepping distance and keeping feet one half shoulder width apart, pointing forward and parallel to each other. Keep your knees loose and slightly bent, and never locked. Walking stance is considered a modern stance and is used extensively in the Taegeuk set of forms and during sparring. Direction changes are simple turns keeping the normal foot spacing we are accustomed to using when standing or walking. Turning is a matter of stepping to the rear with the front foot, while turning on the heel of the rear foot. Make certain that when turning, you move the front foot across the front of your body to maintain normal width spacing, and avoid the fence post alignment (as previously discussed). The other method of turning in place is similar to the back stance. Twist on the heels of your feet, but slide the front foot over slightly to maintain width between your feet, similar to the crabbing effect described in front stance. Remain upright and square to the front at all times. (Fig. 115, 116)

Fighting stance (Moa seogi) is the position you will take when sparring. It is more like the walking stance than any other stance, and allows for fast footwork and rapid execution of kicks and blocks from either side. Take a fighting stance by facing the front while turning your body, hips and feet 45° to the side. From a natural stance facing front, step back with your right leg, feet placed a shoulder width apart and at a 45° angle to the front. Keep your feet parallel to each other. Don't fence post, but maintain some foot width in position and keep weight equally on each foot. Keep hands up in guard position, hands held at face level, elbows tight. Move on the balls of your feet for rapid foot changes and movements in all directions. This stance can be varied for offense or defense, and is often performed with a continuous light jumping. This bouncing motion is done off the balls of the feet, and allows for rapid feet switching and explosive execution of techniques. (Fig. 117)

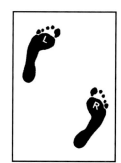

117

The advanced stances start appearing at the higher level Taegeuk and black belt forms, but will usually be learned and used long before you get to those forms. The most common of these is the cat or tiger stance.

Cat stance or tiger stance (Bum seogie) is a shorter stance with about half a shoulder width between the front and rear feet. Body faces to the front. Both legs have bent knees, with 90% of the weight on the rear leg. Rear foot is turned at a 15° angle from the front foot. The front leg holds only 10% of the weight, and is touching the ground only with the ball of the foot. Your heel is lifted off the ground. This is an explosive stance allowing great speed from already coiled muscles. (Fig. 118)

118

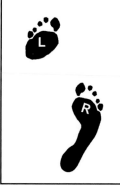

The crane stance (Haktari seogie) is a one legged stance. Stand on one leg, bending it slightly, and place the bottom of your other foot, (specifically the arch), against the inside of your leg just below the knee on the standing leg. This is a surprisingly stable stance for having only one foot on the ground. By slightly lowering your hips, you will lower your center of gravity and add further stability. (Fig. 119)

The X-stance (Kyo cha seogie) is a stance where the shin of one leg is placed or twisted behind the calf of the other leg, usually used after jumping or stepping quickly forward. The front foot is flat on the ground and planted firmly, with the rear foot supported on the ball of the foot. 90% of the weight is on the front leg. Both legs are bent at the knee. Conversely, the stance is also used in a rearward manner, with the front leg stepping or jumping to the rear and twisting across the calf of the rear leg (now in front). (Fig. 120)

KICKING

While Tae Kwon Do teaches the use of all the body's weapons, it is generally considered a kicking style of martial art. Tae Kwon Do distinguishes itself with more kicking techniques and acrobatic maneuvers than other styles. Kicks can account for as much as 80% of Tae Kwon Do techniques.

There are many **ways to use the feet** to execute a kick (Chagie). Like the hands, the particular parts of the foot are more suited to certain attacks than others. It depends on your target—whether it is hard muscle, bones or soft tissue. We also take into consideration that our feet are used more often and in a more demanding way than our hands. We walk, stand, run and jump with them. That strengthens and toughens them. Hundreds or thousands of times a day you set your heel to the ground with your full weight. You step off the ball of your foot when walking, or stand on toes when reaching for something. This daily use, which strengthens and pre-conditions the foot, makes it a natural weapon. We spend a great deal of time conditioning our hands so that we can strike without injuring them. Feet are more naturally ready to kick than hands are to punch. This is simply because feet are used in a similar manner every day.

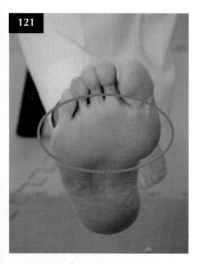

121

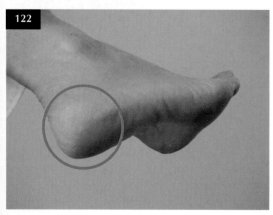

122

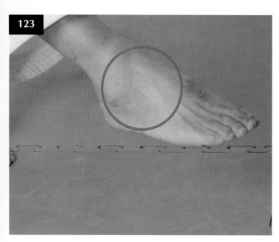

123

The **ball of the foot** (Ap kum chi) is used in executing a front, round-house, or twist kick. The foot is extended forward, with toes pulled back and out of the way so they won't get broken. The position is exactly as if you were to stand on your toes. The instep (top of the foot) is flat and in line with your shin, there is an arch under the bottom of your foot, and the toes stand up at a 45° to 90° angle to the rest of the foot. When striking, use the isolated ball of the foot to make contact. (Fig. 121)

The **heel of the foot** (Dee kum chi) is the hardest and least delicate part of our feet, and we use it for our most powerful kicks—the back kick and sidekick. The heel is also the striking weapon for axe kicks, hook kicks and stomps. When executing a sidekick, the heel aims at the target, with the foot flat and toes pulled back and out of the way. It is important to strike directly with your heel. Newer students often execute this strike with the ball of the foot, or flat footed, and injure the tendon running along the inside bottom of the foot. It's very painful and can cause a serious injury. Use the heel only, as that is the pre-conditioned, least sensitive and thickest skinned portion of the foot. (Fig. 122)

The instep (Bal doong) is the top of the foot and is used for round-house and twist kicks. The instep is made up of numerous small bones, extensions of our toes and the upper foot structure. These bones by themselves are fragile, and the musculature in them delicate; you need to protect them when kicking. That means, when kicking to the ribs, beware of elbows that will break bones and damage your foot. Don't hit hard targets like the shins, knees or forehead. Aim for the front and sides of the face, neck, ribs, stomach region, kidneys, muscular parts of the legs and groin. The instep kicking position of the foot is formed by extending your foot straight out with toes angled down to create a flat surface that is in a straight line with your shin. Your toes should curl down or at least remain flat. The very top of your foot is what strikes the target. The instep kick is usually angular, developing from the side or from an arcing motion. The only time it is used straight on is as a rising kick to the groin, or to the face or body of a bent over person. (Fig. 123)

The **blade**, also known as the **edge of the foot** (Bal nal) is used with a sidekick against the legs, knees, body, kidneys, ribs, face, neck and throat of opponents. It is the outer edge of the foot that hits the target when executing a wheel kick, also known as the outside to inside kick. It is formed by turning the foot over towards its outer edge and pulling the ball up and heel out, with toes tucked under and out of the way. To effectively strike with this kick, forcefully jam the edge of the foot into the targeted area. (Fig. 124)

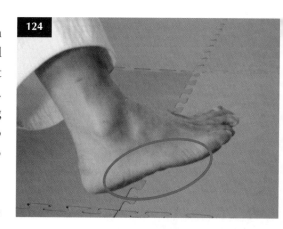

The **bottom of the foot** (Bal ba duke) is used when executing the push kick. It is positioned similarly to the way that you stand on the foot, but try and keep your toes up and out of the way. The foot remains flat and the entire bottom surface strikes the target, with emphasis on the heel. Running into it is like hitting a brick wall when executed properly. It can be both an attack and a defensive strike. The bottom is also the striking surface for the crescent kick, also known as the half moon kick and the outside to inside kick. This kick is an arcing kick that comes across to the body or to the face, and you hit your target with the bottom or arch of the foot since it aligns itself in that direction. Turn the bottom of your foot towards the target so you will not strike fully with the inside edge and damage or injure tendons and ligaments not meant for hard contact. Use it to disarm an attacker with a knife because the entire length of the foot when swung sideways allows a fuller range of contact across the narrow width of an outstretched arm, and it comes in with power enough to break it. (Fig. 125)

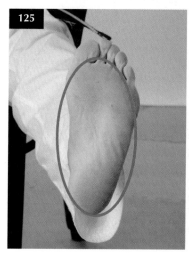

Shins (Ahp jung kang yi) are powerful weapons that can tear into just about any part of the body with the force of a swinging club. Although they stand on their own as a weapon, they are employed or used with a wide variety of kicks. Your shin is the long bone that extends from your knee to your ankle and has a hard ridge on its front. Anatomically, we are speaking about the tibia, the larger of the two bones in our lower leg. (Fig. 126) The shin is a weapon that hard-core martial artists condition to increase bone density, strength and to reduce sensitivity. Practitioners strike padded posts, heavy bags, target pads, and practice breaking techniques with boards and sticks. Breaking baseball bats with shin breaks is one of the most impressive breaking demonstrations of Tae Kwon Do. It's a great weapon to be able to use in defending against an attack. Shins are used with the round-house, twist and rising kick. You can target pretty much any area on the body, from head to toe, and every place and extremity in between.

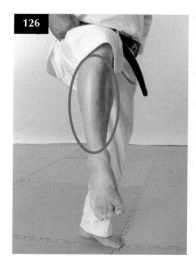

KICKS OF TAE KWON DO

There are many kicks in Tae Kwon Do and, when executed correctly, they strike like lightening. They are as distinctive as they can be effective. Our legs are our largest and most powerful muscle group in our body. The rotational forces produced by our hips and torso when executing these moves further magnifies the power generated by these kicks. The acrobatic aspect makes them difficult to defend against without getting hit. There are four elements to the success of any technique thrown or executed, and all must be present in the one movement:

> **Speed, Power, Accuracy and Timing.**
> Strike a target with power and accuracy, but no speed, and you only push your opponent.
> Strike a target with speed and accuracy, but no power, and you only tap your opponent.
> Strike at a target with speed and power, but no accuracy, and you miss your opponent.

And timing is the over-riding element for the entire move. If you strike too soon, your opponent may not be in the ideal position, or may adjust his attack according to your offensive move. If you strike too late, you will likely be overrun or have your technique cut short. They will beat you to the punch. Timing is the most critical element, and it only develops with practice.

THE KICKS

The front kick (Ap chagi) or **front snap kick** is executed from a fighting, back, walking or front stance. It is executed straight to the front along the centerline with the ball of the foot. Start with the left foot slightly to the

rear in a fighting stance (in this example, the right leg will begin in the front). This kick develops with a raise of the knee and subsequent out-stretching of the lower leg, striking the target with the ball of the foot. It may be executed against the groin or crotch, or a bent over opponent with the instep or shin. For basics we break the kick down to a four count. 1) Shift balance to the front foot and raise your knee. (Fig. 127, 128) 2) Lift the lower portion of the raised leg and kick to target. (Fig. 129) 3) Return the lower portion of the leg to start position with the knee still fully raised. (Fig. 130) 4) Drop knee and step forward into fighting position. (Fig. 131) In this kick, lifting your knee is the critical maneuver to the proper execution of the technique. You can kick to the face and chin, chest, stomach, crotch, thigh, shin, instep. It's all a matter of aiming your knee before the kick, and then executing the kick. For instance, if you don't raise it high enough, you won't kick high. Remember to snap the kick as we discussed earlier in this chapter. Once your knee is raised, snap the lower part of your leg out, pointing the ball of your foot into the target. Make sure the kick penetrates the target, not just striking the sur-face. Drive your hips forward on the release and, to deliver the power, kick as though your target were six inches further than it actually is. Snap quickly, transmitting the power to the target, and remove your leg faster than it went out so it cannot be grabbed. Step back, or forward, and follow up with another technique. There are several important things to keep in mind when executing front kicks. For better balance, the lower part of the kicking leg must be returned fully with the knee still raised high. When kicking, lean forward slightly to generate more power. When you execute your kick, start with the heel lifted off the ground, with only the ball of the foot touching. Keeyup and let out your breath. (Note: You should always let out your breath for each technique, and Keeyup where and when appropriate.)

The **roundhouse** (Ap dolyo chagi) or round kick has its name because it is executed on an angle to the centerline and comes across in a sweeping arc. The kick is effective at a low, medium, or high height, and also works with jumping, spinning, stepping, sliding, and skipping. It has incredible speed and power. The angle may be fully level with the midsection, angling up for high kicks or angling down for low kicks. The kick begins in fighting, walking, front, back, or even horse stance. Start in a fighting stance. Tense your hips for a spring-like snapping reaction when you let loose. The right knee comes up high and your foot and lower portion of the leg rises to become parallel with the ground. (Fig. 132, 133, 134) Aim your knee beyond your target and swing your hips to the left while twisting on the ball of your left foot. Continue the twist of your body as you extend your right leg and somewhat straighten your upper leg, creating a whip-like action and striking with the instep, ball of your foot, or shin. (Fig. 135, 136) Students will learn to maintain their balance on the one leg and execute multiple kicks from the same position, often two, three or more times. Kicks are executed from either the front or rear leg, while you are stepping forward or backward. As with the front kick, return the lower portion of your leg completely to the chambered position before lowering your knee and returning the leg to the ground.

The **sidekick** (Yup chagie) is the most powerful kick in Tae Kwon Do. The sidekick is a heel kick with your entire leg and buttocks muscles. It develops by turning your waist nearly 180° and driving your heel and leg in a rearward motion to your front. The position begins in fighting stance. (Fig. 137) Drop your weight onto a slightly bent lead leg, raise your right knee high, just like a front kick (Fig. 138), but continue in a turning motion so that your knee points 90° to 180° to your left or rear. (Fig. 139) Continue looking to the front, hands held in fighting position for protection and balance. Your leg is raised so it is level or angled upward, and your heel is aimed at the target. Keep your foot level or angled downward with your toes pointed to the floor. Make sure the left leg you are standing on is bent for balance, and that your heel is pointed towards your target. Snap your hips and leg fully out and strike the target (Fig. 140), immediately pulling back to the previous position with your leg still raised. Your foot travels straight out and back along the same line. (Fig. 141) Return by twisting your hips and body 180° back to your starting position, twisting on the ball of your standing foot and replacing the kicking leg back to where you started. (Fig. 142) This is a difficult kick to execute properly. For that reason, it's taught from the very beginning, allowing you to develop flexibility, balance, speed, power, accuracy and proper form. When executed correctly, sidekicks are a speedy one kick takeout.

A simple five count can be used to further illustrate the execution of this kick. 1) Knee comes up. 2) Knee and leg cross in front of your

137

138

139

body with a twisting motion, aligning your heel with target. 3) Kick heel straight towards target. 4) Return leg to same chambered position as in step number two. 5) Return to fighting stance, by turning body back to start position and placing kicking leg to the rear. Please keep in mind that once you have learned the basic one-two count, moves one and two are executed as one rapid movement. Speed and fluidity of motion are essential.

For more power, maintain tension or tight muscles on the side of your kicking leg to generate more explosive power. Sidekicks can be executed with either leg, and with both the front and rear leg. It is executed from front, back, walking, fighting and horse stance. They are performed as a stepping technique, offensively as well as defensively, and with variations. Flying sidekicks start with a single step, or short run, and then go straight into a jump, turning in mid air towards the target. The force of this strike would knock a man off a horse, and allegedly that was one of its original uses. We will explore the progression of difficulty of these kicks from basic through jump spinning back sidekick later in this book.

As you gain proficiency with this kick, you will learn to raise your knee and twist your body in one motion without the basic one-two chambering and rear facing position for greater speed. It will be executed in a swift fluid motion so that as you begin to align your leg with your target, your hips will turn but the knee will remain to the front, executing the kick in a single motion.

The **back sidekick** is a variation on the previously described side-kick, and is executed to your back side, or as a rear turning kick. From the same fighting stance as the sidekick (Fig. 143), look over your right shoulder, and turn your body to the rear. Aim the heel of your front leg (left) directly at your target for accuracy. (Fig. 144) Bend your knees slightly and raise your right leg (Fig. 145) kicking straight back (directly to the front where you faced) and drive into the target with your heel. (Fig. 146) You can either return your kicking leg to the original starting position or leave it in front. (Fig 147) If you leave the kicking leg in the front, you will have to make adjustments to your body position, but the circumstances will determine the appropriate choice when the time comes. For practice, execute this kick both ways, and with both legs, developing skill equally on both sides.

A **back kick** (Dwit chagi) is what we refer to as a mule kick. It is similar to the sidekick in development and execution, but it is aimed to the rear and does not require you to change your body position or direction. In the back kick, the heel of the non-kicking leg is raised off the ground and points towards the target. The knee of the kicking leg is not raised as high as the sidekick, so execution is quicker. It can be executed as a blind kick if you become aware of an attacker behind you, or you can sneak a peak for accuracy. Start from the position of a ready stance, feet shoulders width apart. Bend your knees slightly (Fig. 148), glance over your shoulder on the same side as you kicking leg (Fig. 149), shift your weight to the standing leg and raise your free leg slightly to kicking position. (Fig. 150), This time, kick straight back while leaning slightly forward. Note that it is perfectly acceptable to raise the leg and execute this kick like a sidekick, but straight to your rear. (Fig. 151) Return to your original position while keeping an eye on target if appropriate. (Fig. 152, 153) When kicking, drive straight to the rear with the heel, kicking more than once if necessary. You may use either foot, and may alternate, kicking once with each. Let your breath out with each kick.

The **wheel kick** (Hwe jun chagi), also known as the inside to outside kick, the half moon kick and the inside axe kick, is an arcing circular kick that moves across the center line towards the outside of your body. Start in fighting stance. (Fig. 154) Turn your front foot (left) slightly to the left. Shift your weight to that foot, drop your hips on the right side and swing your right leg to the outside while raising it in front of your body to the left of centerline (Fig. 155), as it moves up and inwardly across. (Fig. 156) As it rises, begin to change direction so it now swings right of centerline at face level, and continues through, down and back to starting position, landing right foot back. Extend your hip into the kick as it rises, providing the snap of power to knock a person down. The strike occurs at face level with the outer edge or side of your heel hitting the side of opponent's face (in this case, the right side of the face). (Fig. 157) Wheel kicks can be thrown from the front or side of your opponent. They are a competition technique that is executed with great speed, particularly when spinning, or turning to the rear to execute. It's really hard to see them develop in competition because they happen so fast with today's competitors.

The **crescent kick** (Pyojeok chagi), also known as the target kick, the outside to inside kick and the outside axe kick, starts to the right of centerline, and crosses over. Starting in fighting stance, extend and open flat your left hand in front of you to act as the target. (Fig. 158), Twist your front foot (left) outward slightly while swinging your right leg out (Fig. 159), up and over the centerline at face level while maintaining an upright position. Swing it to your outstretched hand (simulating your opponent's head) and strike with the bottom of the foot or side of the heel. Turn your hips in the direction of the kick for power. (Fig. 160) Return foot to starting position, or step down to the front. Hold your other hand high for protection throughout the entire technique. This technique is particularly good for attacking assailants wielding weapons, as it can easily knock a weapon in someone's hand aside, creating an opening for an immediate counter attack. It can be executed with a jump, and a series of kicks can be strung together with stepping turns, and as jump turning kicks, one after another after another.

The **axe kick** (Buder chagie) is a high kick, delivering power in a downward motion. In the time another martial arts stylist might take a step forward, a Tae Kwon Do stylist can step forward and deliver the axe. Starting in fighting stance, raise your rear leg, straightening it as it rises straight up, above head height and as high as you can. Lean forward while dropping and driving the leg down onto your opponent's head, neck, shoulder, collar bone or back. (Fig. 161, 162, 163, 164, 165) Reset your kicking leg as needed, or step down in front and deliver a second kick with your other leg. It's a driving technique that can move an opponent back. Moving an opponent backwards presents an advantage to you because a person can without a doubt move forward faster than they can backward. In driving the opponent back, you can create the opportunity to close the distance with your opponent and overcome them. Axe kicks strike downward with the back or bottom of the heel.

The **push kick** (Mil a chagi) is a kick directly to your front with the bottom of your foot. It's an effective way to check or cut the action of your opponent, or drive home a vicious attack to the midsection. At worst, it will get your opponent off balance, creating an advantage that allows you to counter attack. The push kick is a forward driving frontal stomp with the bottom of your foot. Starting in fighting stance, raise your back leg and knee all the way to your chest or shoulder with the toes raised and pulled back. (Fig. 166) Push your leg directly to the front, and push off hard with your grounded leg. Lead your kick with the flat of your right heel. (Fig. 167) Drive the kicking leg straight forward and, once the kick is completed, place it to the front. You may then rush forward towards a back staggering opponent and execute a finishing technique. This can be a follow-up kick, punch, or combination of what you choose and what the circumstances allow. Variation on this technique is angular execution. For example, if you execute this kick as just described, you can tilt your right leg to the left and use a modification that is a combination of a front kick and sidekick. Do whatever works for you, circumstances allowing. Variations on angles and executions of Tae Kwon Do moves that work are acceptable so long as they are effective and practical in their application.

The **twist kick** (Biteuro chagi) may be the least used and most under-rated kick in Tae Kwon Do. It is sometimes called a reverse roundhouse. It is fast, powerful and deceptive. Twist kicks are best executed from the open stance. In other words, if you stand with your right foot forward, and so does your opponent, then you are standing in a closed stance. An open stance means that you have the opposite foot forward as your opponent. So, if you stand in what appears to be a mirror image of your opponent, you are standing in the open stance. You don't have to stand opposite sided. Twist kicks can be thrown from either the front or rear leg. Front leg kicks are naturally faster to execute. In Tae Kwon Do, we are constantly moving on our feet, dancing around, jumping lightly and switching our forward facing side, trying to confuse our opponents so we can create an opening to exploit. We use feints or false moves to entice the opponent to take a step forward or backward; whatever will create an opening where we can have an advantage for attack. The twist kick is one of those great surprises that too many Tae Kwon Do students never get to use. It is swift and close to your opponent for rapid contact. A twist kick is a reverse roundhouse in execution. Standing with your right foot forward, drop your weight to the rear (left) leg, while also dropping your right hip and taking weight off the right leg. Turn your right knee to the outside while raising it and twisting the lower portion of your leg from inside the centerline and extending it up and outside, striking with the shin, instep or ball of the foot. Twist kicks can be delivered with either the front or rear leg, and directed to the front or sides. Target areas are the face, head, ribs, chest, abdomen, groin, arms and legs. (Fig. 168, 169, 170, 171)

The **hook kick** (Ban Dal Chagie) and the spinning hook kick are the farthest reaching kicks, meaning the fully extended length of your leg. These are probably the kicks young kids want to emulate the most after seeing them used in so many movies. Hook kicks are a reverse kick that crosses centerline and attacks on the way back across it. Begin in fighting stance. Raise your right leg as you would for a roundhouse but point your knee fully to your left, twisting on the ball of your foot, and reach it across your front towards your left. Extend the lower portion of your leg while directing your heel and foot towards the target in a circular motion that crosses back over to the right side of the centerline, ideally at head level. Arc your leg across and back towards your right side, replacing your leg and foot in the starting position. As you draw the foot across the target area, drive your thigh and hip back to add snap and generate power. Snap your lower leg back to maximize power and speed with the kick. (Fig. 172, 173, 174, 175, 176)

The **spinning hook kick** is the same technique, executed while turning to your rear. Begin in fighting stance, look to the rear over your right shoulder, while turning your front foot (left) 180° to the rear. Bend your left knee and take the bulk of your weight onto your left leg. While continuing your turning motion to the rear, raise your right leg and execute the hook kick as described above, swinging it fully around after striking the target to land in its original position. Your foot will travel in a 360° arc, extending out and striking to the front where directed. Hook kicks can be executed with the front or rear leg, and while spinning to the rear. (Fig. 177, 178, 179, 180, 181, 182)

PUNCHING (CHIRUGIE)

Ways to use hands

The name Tae Kwon Do describes the primary weapons that we use in our style. Tae Kwon Do means "the way of the feet and hands". Literally, "Tae" means foot, "Kwon" means hand, and "Do" means "the Art" or "the Way". In this chapter, we will take a look at the many ways of using our hands, and the techniques and strikes that make them effective.

Our **hands** (Sahn), the appendages that physically separate us from the rest of the animal kingdom, are a complex assortment of bone, tissue and sinew that has created some of the most beautiful pieces of art on our planet. Hands have created great works of literature, beautiful paintings, moving sculptures, and the intricate movements in dance of various cultures around the world. Hands also possess the ability to generate great power and force when necessary and when applied in a martial way. The martial hand is the hand of Tae Kwon Do, and it is this hand that we will now discuss.

Our hands can be shaped in numerous ways, some very effective for martial arts techniques. Some parts of the hand are too delicate to strike or defend with, so proper hand technique is important.

Making a **fist** (Ju mok) is technically more complex than it first appears. When making a proper fist, open the hand flat. (Fig. 183) Start with the finger tips of the four fingers, bending the finger tips as tightly together as possible. (Fig. 184) Next, bend these four fingers and roll them onto your palm as tightly as possible. (Fig. 185) Then roll your thumb onto your folded fingers and close it all like a ball of steel. (Fig. 186) To be sure that you have formed a proper fist, make certain that each part of the fist is tight and without excess movement. (Fig. 187) You will prevent loss of power due to excess finger movement or flexing, and you have a better chance of avoiding injury. Tae Kwon Do fists are used by striking straight to the front with the two large knuckles of your folded fist. Your wrist should be slightly angled to the side so that these two knuckles align with your forearm. This will strengthen your punch and help to avoid a sprained wrist. Your fists, when used correctly, are one of your primary weapons—they are powerful, direct, and fast.

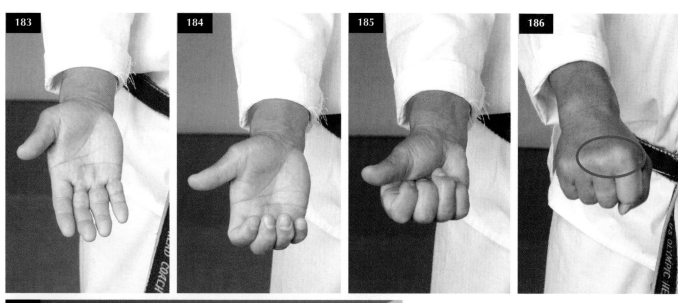

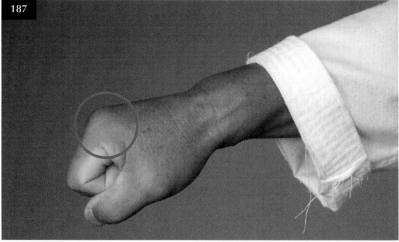

The **hammer-fist** (Me ju mok) (Fig. 188) is used in an arcing or spinning motion, striking with the pinkie side of the hard fist of your hand. (Fig. 189, 190) This is a particularly powerful weapon and its effectiveness depends on speed and accuracy. It can be used against most any part of the body.

A **back-fist** (Deung ju mok) (Fig. 191) is use of the hand in a fist, with the two large knuckles on top portion of your hand making the contact for the strike. Execution is with the top of the hand facing towards the target. (Fig. 192)

The **knife-hand** (Son nal) is one of the most frequently used offensive and defensive weapons. It is a flat-handed position where the four fingers are fully extended, but slightly bent and pressed together, looking similar to the universally recognized "stop" signal. Your thumb is flat against the side of your hand, but the tip is slightly bent onto the palm side for strength, support, and to avoid injury. Knife-hands are used for neck chops and various blocks by attacking with the thick part on the outside side of your hand. (Fig. 193)

By adjusting your fingertips slightly to bring the finger lengths even, your hand is now in what is called the **spear-hand** position. This is used as a forward thrust for jabbing or spearing into soft tissue areas of the body such as the neck and solar plexus. (Fig. 194, 195)

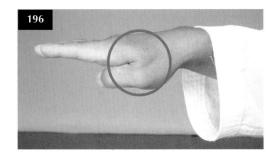

A **ridge-hand** (Yok son kahl) uses the thumb side of the hand, and specifically the small triangle made by the thumb and side of the hand beside your thumb. This technique is excellent for strikes to the neck, face, and ribs, and can easily be slid beneath a punch to cut short the action of your attacker. (Fig. 196)

The **palm-heel** (Pa tang son) is used to attack the side of the face and jaw, the torso ribs and groin, or to block a developing punch or kick. It is made by placing your hand in a position similar to the "stop" sign, but with your forearm straight out from your body, and the hand at a 90° angle to the arm. Fingers are pulled all the way up and out of harms way. In palm-heel, the thumb remains beside the other fingers so it is not injured when striking. The contact point for the strike is with the meaty portion of the bottom of your palm. This eliminates the wrist flexibility that might cause your hand and arm to fold up during a powerful punch. It is a closer strike by the length of the fist or fingers. It is a devastating blow when done correctly, with great stopping force and full projection of power. (Fig. 197)

The **bear paw** is a bent finger strike using the knuckles of the first joint of each of the four fingers to strike with. Start as if you were forming a fist. When the four fingers are bent over tightly, with the hand still flat, press your thumb against the side of your hand tightly. Strike straight forward and hit with your projecting bent knuckles. This strike is used against soft tissue targets such as the throat. Bear paws can extend your striking reach by the length of about 3 inches beyond a hard fist. (Fig. 198)

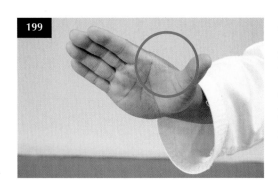

An **arc hand** (Ah kum sahn), also known as the fork hand, is used by creating a "V" like formation between your thumb and the main four fingers of your hand. Start as if you were forming a knife-hand, but rather than pressing your thumb to the side, open it outward to create the fork. Bend your four fingers slightly and send power to your hand. This technique is used mainly against your opponent's exposed neck, or to block a strike or weapon attack. (Fig. 199)

Slaps are a more dangerous type of attack than most people realize. A lot of people commonly assume that a slap is not powerful. Though executed with the flat of an open hand, skilled Tae Kwon Do practitioners can break bricks and concrete slabs with slaps. A slap can kill a person if directed with enough power. Always remember that there are no "gentle" strikes. If somebody slaps you, make no mistake about it, you have been attacked, and do not let it happen a second time. Walk away, block it, defend against it if the situation requires, but do not just stand there. Slaps can be used for attacks, but are used just as often as a block, a slapping away technique, or parrying. Deflection of an attack is just as good, and sometimes better, than a full contact block; it is often less painful and you are less likely to get hurt. (Fig. 200)

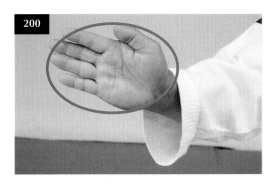

Extended knuckles of the hand present a clear message to your enemy, a message that says, "Prepare for pain". When making a fist, extend the first knuckle of your middle finger (Bamchu ju mok) of your fist so the knuckle protrudes out from, and yet is supported by, the other fingers. An uppercut to the ribs where the knuckle can partially penetrate between them will instantly disrupt your opponent's attack. Make sure the hand is tight and that you do not strike to hard body parts, as that could injure the finger. (Fig. 201)

Similarly, the **thumb knuckle** fist (Oomji ju mok) can be supported against the side of the hand and swung in an arc against the ribs, neck, jaw and temple. You are more vulnerable to injury if this technique is used incorrectly than you are with other techniques. Use it rarely, practice it often, and become a specialist before using it. (Fig. 202)

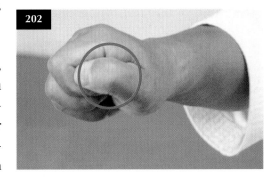

HAND STRIKES are so varied they help create an arsenal that, when combining punches and kicks in three move combinations, you have more than 3,000 possibilities. Different circumstances will determine which is appropriate and right for you at any given moment. For example, in defending against an attack from a threatening but non-lethal aggressor, you will more likely interrupt his attack and restrain him, as opposed to causing severe injury or worse. An attack may be directed against a less vulnerable body target, or with less ferocity. Again, this is the concept of "level of escalation" (as discussed in the chapter on Tae Kwon Do's philosophy). Use what force is necessary, not an automatic full throttle response. Again, this depends upon the circumstances of the confrontation.

A proper punch or kick starts with what we call a "fold" prior to the execution. In a middle punch, while in ready, horse riding or front leaning stance, the right hand is pulled all the way to the belt, and the opposite (left) hand is extended out in front. (Fig. 203) The punch develops power in several ways: Power is developed through tensing of the hips and rotating them at the same time as you pull the extended left hand toward the left belt. At the same time, twist your right wrist and thrust forward with your right hand. (Fig. 204, 205) Your punching hand is rotated so that, having started with your fist facing palm up at your side, you extend the punch and rotate so your palm is face down when the punch is completed. (Fig. 206) The fold is also a power creating technique, which is quite scientific in principle. Imagine that in the punching position just described, you actually hold a length of rope in each hand, but the center is strung through a pulley mechanism. Step back to take up the slack, and as you punch with the right hand, pull your extended left hand towards you. Reverse the punch, and your other hand returns to you. By using this principle, you magnify power through a fuller range of motion and by adding rotational power to the overall movement.

Rotational power brings more of your body into the execution of a move by allowing power to be added by sequentially combining one movement element immediately after the previous. For example, in a simple punch from your side to the middle, simply twisting your wrist into the punch doubles the power. Your wrist provides this additional power. Now, fold as described and punch, and you will add the rotating power from your entire shoulder cage, of both sides together, again doubling power. Now add a rotation and rapid twist of the hips, and power is again magnified by about double. And when we add leg power, we produce a punch that has been magnified in power many times and, when perfected, is a devastating weapon.

Breathing is critical to your power and centeredness. And of course we all know the EEEIIIAAAYYHHHHH, a loud yell called a Kie-hap or Keeyup. Keeyups are loud shouts that begin from the belly and rapidly

expel air from the lungs. It is a technique that serves several purposes, not the least of which is scaring the heck out of your opponent. It is a shout of confidence as well as a breathing and power generating technique. Sports trainers and exercise physiologists all teach breathing techniques during their training sessions. The martial arts relies upon breath for reasons that include centeredness, meditation, healing exercises, and for control of emotion and pain, just to mention a few. Breathing allows you to fuel your muscles and control your body. Holding your breath restricts your abilities. Always allow for a smooth deep breathing to maximize your physical and mental abilities. Breathing exercises are practiced in many schools, and your breath development will improve through your training.

There are several ways we execute a punch or kick, primarily by **snapping** or **thrusting**. A snapping punch is extremely fast and leaves its power behind by transmitting the power into the target at its peak of generation. When executed properly, this is the technique used to "suck out" the lit flame on candles. When executing this punch, at the apex or end of the actual punch, tense your muscles and pull back twice as fast as you made the punch. This is done at the very end, and pulls or sucks your fist back several inches. It conserves and amplifies power at the same time. However, properly executing a snap does take a while to get the hang of. A thrusting kick, compared to a snapping kick, drives hard through the target, and does not have the snap or slight pull back at the end. It is also a devastating technique, but harder on the joints. It is more beneficial to train and spar with snapping kicks and punches.

Hand striking techniques

The first punch taught is a **jab**. A jab is nothing more than a straight punch, usually to your opponent's face or head. Get into fighting position, hands up for protection, left foot slightly forward, teeth clenched, and chin tucked towards your lead (left) shoulder. Your legs are slightly bent, and you are relaxed. Your hands are held high, close to your face, with elbows down and close in to protect your ribs. Your jab will develop from your lead shoulder or ear (Fig. 207), and with a slight rotating motion of your wrist, punch straight out (Fig. 208), and return right back to your original position. (Fig. 209) Let some breath out as you punch so that your energy will flow. This punch is also called a lead or lead-hand jab.

A **reverse jab** would be executed with your opposite, or right hand, left foot forward. It is also executed straight out (Fig. 210) and back to your guarded hands up position. The old one-two is a jab, followed by a reverse jab in quick succession.

The next technique is a **middle punch** (Momtong chirugie). In formal practice this punch is executed from a front, walking or horse stance. It is executed on the same side as your lead leg. It develops from your waist and attacks the center of your opponent, or the solar plexus region. When practicing, try to face a mirror and aim for your own center. This will mean that, when executing the punch, you must angle slightly downward and towards your centerline to make contact with your opponent's middle or solar plexus region. (Fig. 211)

A **reverse punch** (Ban deh chirugie) is identical to the middle punch except that it starts on the opposite side of the body, on the rear leg side. Using the hand opposite your lead leg is a reverse punch. (Fig. 212)

A **high punch** (Olgul chirugie) is the same as the middle punch, but targets the face and head. Realistically, your target could be to the point on the upper lip below the nose called the philtrum, the eyes, the jaw, perhaps even the throat. You may also use a fork hand to the throat, or bear paw to the philtrum. A low punch would target the groin or lower abdomen. You have numerous choices, all derived from this basic punch. (Fig. 213)

Armpit attacks are often side-stepping attacks to the outside of your attacker, and drive a fist (Fig. 214) or spear-hand directly up and into the armpit. (Fig. 215) The disruption to the brachial nerve can cause immediate numbness. The extreme case of this attack is death.

Double punches (Doo bun chirugie) are a series of two punches in quick succession, first with one hand (Fig. 216), then the other. (Fig. 217) They can both be executed low, middle or high, or one of each in any order. Multiple punches of three (Sae bun chirugie), four and even ten are the same, just in rapid-fire motion while alternating punching hands. These are sometimes referred to as "flurries" of punches. They can be thrown to the body or head.

Back-fists (Deung ju mok) are executed using a fist with the back of the hand facing your opponent, and striking with the two large knuckles on the top of the hand. It is executed from various positions, but the movement is usually forward or to the sides. (Fig. 218, 219)

A **hook-punch** (Gullgi chirugie) is a sweeping punch that starts from a fighting position, and swings outward, arcing towards the target, usually with the lead hand, and striking from the side. When you are fighting close in, they are difficult to see, and often a set-up for a follow-up strike or blow. (Fig. 220, 221)

Uppercuts (Ju mok jeochyo chirugie) are upward thrusting punches that develop from the waist and curve upwards and to the front. They are also used angularly by stepping to the outside and striking exposed ribs. They are hard to see coming and are often part of a multi-punch flurry of different types. One example would be a combination of a jab, uppercut, hook, jab and reverse punch. Should your opponent drop their hands when hit with an uppercut, the hook will find him or her open and they'll get hit, probably more than once. Multi-strike moves give you the best chance of connecting with your enemy and ending a confrontation. (Fig. 222, 223)

The **spear-hand** (Pyonson keut chirugie or Kwan soo) is well named because of how it is used. From your side, or close in to your body, make your hand into the shape of the knife-hand as discussed above (flattened and with extended fingers), and thrust strongly towards the soft tissue areas of your attacker. Literally spear forward to your target, with the thumb side of your hand up. (Fig. 224, 225) Attack the neck, throat, solar plexus, groin, armpit, and even face. This is a penetrating technique, also effective when attacking the ribs. The shocking penetration of the blow which results can disrupt the functioning of vital organs. It can interrupt arterial blood flow, temporarily disabling your opponent, and create an opportunity for further attack or withdrawal. The spear-hand allows you to reach several inches further than with a fist, but overall, it sacrifices some power due to fingers being less strong than a tight fist. One nasty technique that completely takes the fight out of an opponent is to spear thrust upward, with palm facing up, to the underside of the rib cage. It is just like an uppercut. The shock to internal organs is immediate and will rapidly take the fight out of your enemy. To make this technique more extreme, you can actually grab the ribs from underneath, hanging on and terrorizing your enemy, should the situation so require (note that this does not work well on overweight people because their ribs are too well padded).

224

225

Neck chops (Son nal mok chigie) are the famed "Karate chops" of movie legend. They are knife-hand attacks executed with a chopping motion, targeting the neck, collarbone, face, torso or appendages. Begin with right knife-hand held near the right ear, and slice across aiming the thick portion of your hand at the target with the palm up. Neck attacks are especially dangerous, and should never be practiced on your training partners, except in slow motion. Make sure, as with all techniques, that you never use great force or power while executing a technique that might hurt your partner. (Fig. 226, 227)

Reverse knife-hand starts by reaching your flattened hand to your opposite side, and striking with the thick side of your hand and with the palm facing down or to the outside. Start by bringing your left hand to your right ear, and strike towards center line and your opponent's neck. (Fig. 228, 229)

Double-fist attacks (Doo ju mok chirugie) are introduced at a more advanced level, and use both fists together to attack the opponent. In front stance, horse riding stance, back stance or X-stance, the fists simultaneously strike the target, doubling the impact and body shock. Examples are the double uppercut (Sosum chirugie), (Fig. 230, 231), U or C shaped punch, high-low (Dikootja chirugie), diamond shaped punch (Keumgang chirugie), and wing shaped punch (Nalgeh chirugie).

The **swallow-form** (Jebi poom) **knife-hand strike** (Son nal mak chigi) is two moves rolled into one. It is a high block combined with a knife-hand neck chop, thus blocking and attacking in a single motion. (Fig. 232, 233)

Forearm (Pal mok) attacks are not the most common in Tae Kwon Do, but they are effective for close quarters fighting, and if they're good enough to block with, they're good enough to attack with. At times, you might find yourself in a sort of dead zone, where you're too close for one technique and too far for another. There's always the opportunity to improvise, and forearms, like shins, have a place in your arsenal. We can use both the inner forearm (Fig. 234) and the outer forearm. (Fig. 235)

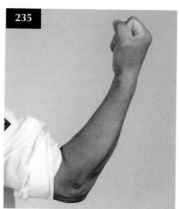

BLOCKS (Magkie) are your first line of defense, after avoiding or evading an attack. It is recommended that you slip, sidestep, shed, deflect or duck an attack rather than meeting it head on. Sometimes you just can't stop the onrush of an attacker's power, so you have to make adjustments accordingly. But why would you stand still if you can step out of the line of attack and avoid an undesirable clash? In evading attacks, the concept of a centerline of attack will help you understand how best to avoid them. To learn this concept, you should stand in ready stance, facing to the front with your feet about one shoulder width apart. Imagine a centerline running from you to the attacker directly in front of you. As you move, so moves your centerline. It is always in the direction you face. Your ready stance straddles this line. Your attacker, when rushing in for a middle punch, will focus on your center. If you quickly step behind your left foot with right foot, and cross over, your attacker will rush past you without making contact. It's a similar technique used in bull fighting. We call it a "step behind" and it's a basic evasion technique. You can do the same thing by stepping across in front, and crossing your centerline (step through). You must wait until your attacker is practically upon you, otherwise he will simply adjust his direction of attack. This same concept works for angular evasions, stepping further outside the centerline and removing the bulk of your body from harms way. This is illustrated in the way that boxers constantly move their feet, heads and body. Partly this is because it's harder to hit a moving target, and your head is the easiest body part to get out of harms way. Speed and footwork is the equalizing factor for boxers, and it's also critical for martial artists. Just think: If you were fast enough to get away from every technique thrown at you, you wouldn't even need to learn how to block.

But there are plenty of times we have to do both at once, side step or angle step to the front, and deflect a punch, kick, or counter as appropriate. So we must develop our blocking ability to protect ourselves, even if it's only needed for an instant. It's easy to block what we see coming, but even then, as noted above, some techniques you are better off avoiding. Blocking a well-practiced martial artist's front kick may deflect and protect your body from the kick, but it might also break your arm simply from the impact and shock of the kick's power. Complete avoidance, or a deflection, may better serve your purpose. Now, let's look at the blocks and a brief explanation of how each is executed.

The **down block** (Areh magkie), also known as the low blocks, is performed to defend the lower portion of the body and legs. It can be executed to the front, the sides and at angles in between. It is executed with a closed fist and swings in a downward arc toward the outside of the body and across the centerline. Low blocks clear a path with your fist and forearm across the lower body from one side to the other. We use both hands, and a folding motion, to create rotational power. This single action is one of the most awkward motions to learn when beginning your training in Tae Kwon Do. It will require practice to develop the neural pathway of motion for this block, but soon it will feel totally natural. Start in front stance (in this example, as with the other examples in this section, with your left leg forward) with your hands in fists. Raise your left fist to your right ear (palm to the ear), while keeping the elbow close to your body. Move your right hand and arm, which are angled down and towards your left side, out in front of you, aligning it with the left side of your body, in the down block fold position. In this position, both your arms are aligned on an angle in front of your chest. (Fig. 236) The next two motions are done at the same time. Sweep your left arm from your right ear down towards your left thigh, while pulling your right hand to your right waist and turning the palm up. You are now standing with the block complete. (Fig. 237) A sweeping block like this will clear a wide path in front of you, so if a punch was aimed at your lower belly, you can, with the correct speed and timing, knock it away from center line and avoid being hit. For a counter-attack, use your right hand; it has already been brought to your waist, so it is cocked and ready to throw a counter-punch.

236

237

The **inner block** (Momtong magkie), also known as the inner middle block or inside block, is used to deflect attacks to areas between the middle and upper body. This motion starts with one arm (in this example it is the right arm to right ear) raised to your ear on the same side, palm out and elbow up. A fold for power is done with the other (left) arm raised in front of you, the hand in a fist with the palm down. The right hand strikes from the right ear towards the centerline and across it with an arcing motion. (Fig. 238) The elbow is kept low, the fist upright, and the block slices sideways and across your body. You only have to pass slightly through centerline to deflect an oncoming punch towards the outside and away from your body. (Fig. 239) This motion, from either side of the body, is a sweeping forearm motion that clears a path in front of your upper torso and head with your hand at face level. Inner blocks can also be executed with a knife-hand or a palm hand for targeted deflections, such as against a knife attack. The actual contact point of your block can be made with your hand or forearm.

Outer blocks (Bakat magkie), also know as an outer middle and outside middle block, protect the same area as inside blocks, but these blocks start from the opposite side of the body. To remember more easily: An inner block is executed from the outside of the centerline to inside, whereas an outer block is from inside of the centerline to the outside. Inner and outer vary, depending on the arm being used, but the execution is the same, just in mirror image. Outer blocks start by reaching one hand towards the waist on your opposite side (in this example, it is your left hand down towards your right waist). (Fig. 240) Then, circle up and to the left across your body, hand up with the palm facing towards your chest, and passing across your chest to the outside of your body to the left side. Hand is brought to face level to protect against face attacks. The fold starts with your left hand at your right side. Your right hand is folded by putting it straight out in front, and is pulled to your hip simultaneously with the execution of your block. (Fig. 241)

Rising blocks (Olgul magkie), also known as high blocks, sweep from low and drive upwards, clearing your frontal region from the waist to just above your head. Your forearm will be held at a slight angle above horizontal. Take your hand, place it by your opposite (right) hip and raise the arm and fist, so that you end up with your left fist above the right side of your head, turning it palm out. It's used to block attacks from above, and the motion generates the power needed to keep a downward strike from a hand, arm or stick from crushing your skull, neck or collarbone. It almost looks like a punch starting from your right hip with the left hand, and punching into the upper right quadrant above your head. Your left hand stays on your right side the entire time. Your forearm ends up about one fist in width above your head, and one fist in front of your face. The forearm is slightly angled, so downward attacks will be deflected away from your head or

face (if your arm is level, the strike may break your arm, and drive through it onto your skull). (Fig. 242, 243) In this block the fold starts with the hand that has just high blocked. Your forearm and hand are turned vertically with your palm turned towards your face, hand up, and elbow down, but directly to the front and in your center line. It literally blocks your center line from head to chest. Your blocking hand moves from your hip to above your head while the folding hand drops to the hip on the side that the block originated on.

The **knife-hand blocks** (Sonal magkie) are executed with hands in the flat, knife-hand position. Aside from being able to use a knife-hand for inner and outer blocks, each knife-hand technique develops a little differently. There are single and double knife-hand blocks, executed low, to center or face level. Single knife-hand starts while standing in a back stance (in this example, left leg is forward), the left hand in knife shape, reaches back and starts at the right ear, palm flat to ear. Execute by twisting the hand to the front while bringing the entire arm forward to centerline, keeping the elbow down and close to your side. The striking edge is the thick outer part of the hand, which is the same part used for a neck chop. This technique blocks and deflects frontal attacks and, additionally positions the hand for wrist grabs. (Fig. 244, 245)

The double knife-hand employs both hands simultaneously. The left hand motion stays exactly the same. We add the right hand and have a double knife-hand as follows: Again, starting in back stance, (in this example, the left leg is forward), right arm extends level and directly to the rear with the palm down and the hand in knife position. Pull the right hand to the front of your chest, while turning the palm up. End with the thick edge of your right hand cupped under your left breast, with your fingers extended slightly beyond your body. Left hand blocks at the same time when it is extended in front of you. (Fig. 246, 247)

246

247

The **scissors block** (Gawi magkie) is a more advanced double arm block of great usefulness. Most martial artists will attack with multiple techniques, and combinations, one kick or punch after another. Many use two at the same time. A scissors block allows defense against such an attack, by blocking in a circular motion with both arms at once. It is basically an outer block and a down block with opposite hands, making it appear as though there is a scissoring motion. (Fig. 248, 249)

The **diamond block** (Keumgang momtong magkie) is another dual block, which begins from back stance and combines the outer block and high block with opposite hands to the outside of the body. (Fig. 250, 251)

The **double fist middle block** (Geodeureo momtong magkie), or low block (Geodeureo areh magkie), is executed very much like knife-hand blocks, except that the hands are in fists. It can be executed in the "supported style" (ideal for massive attacks, such as kicks) by having the rear fist press against the forearm of the forward arm. (Fig. 252, 253)

The **mountain blocks** (Santeul magkie) are executed with one arm (Oe santeul magkie) (Fig. 254) or both and in a variety of stances. A mountain block is a raised arm block, upper arm extended level and

254

straight out to the side. The elbow is bent, the forearm is upright, the hand in a fist and the palm is turned towards the body. It can be executed from the front to the rear or from rear to the front. The block always finishes with arms out to the side. Double mountain blocks can be executed in opposite directions, one arm to the front, one to the rear, or both to the rear as shown below. (Fig. 255)

255

X-blocks (Eot georeo magkie) are superb for stopping kicks or overhead attacks, and trapping the opponent at the same time. X-blocks are executed by overlapping your forearms at the wrist, hands in fists, one over the other to make an "X" pattern. Blocking will start from your hip on one side or another, hands already crossed. Aim to intercept a low front kick or punch by catching it in the "V" formed by the hands at the wrist, and abruptly cutting the action. (Fig. 256, 257) For an overhead attack, the same execution is used. Aim from your hip to generate power, and trap the attacking hand in the fork of your overlaid hands. Additional technique may be applied from the "catch" position in the form of a grab, throw or restraining lock. (Fig. 258, 259)

Palm blocks (Pa tang son an magkie) are applied with the hand in palm heel position. You aim for an extended hand or limb with the flat palm of your hand, fingers drawn up and back, and strike with the heel of the palm. It's the thickest part of your hand and naturally the toughest. This will deflect a punch or knife attack, and allow a counter motion for your attack, or perhaps a wrist grab. (Fig. 260, 261) This block can be angular in direction, or from across the body while stepping off and away from centerline. It can be used directly to the front, such as to the solar plexus or jaw (Fig. 262), and is also useful to prevent a clinch. A double palm block to your attacker's shoulders as he or she charges in to tackle you will stop or cut their action. A follow-up such as a knee to face or chest would be appropriate.

Double forearm wedging blocks (Hechuh magkie), also known simply as wedging blocks or spreading blocks, are used against an attacker trying to grab your face, head, lapels or perhaps to defend against a double neck chop. You must be very fast since this usually defends against a close range attack. Quickly bring both hands to face level, crossed at the wrist with palms facing chest, and hands held close to your chest. Explode with power while outer blocking both hands at the same time, and turning both wrists forward in the process. Your hands are now inside your attacker's, creating opportunities for counter attacks, such as a head grab with knee smash as a follow up. (Fig. 263, 264)

The **concentration push** (Tong Milgi) as we first see used in the Poomse Koryo, starts in the Jhoom-be Jhase (ready stance). In the concentration push, focus your mental concentration by positioning the hand in between the upper and lower abdomen where "sin" (divine) and "jeong" (spirit) converge. This is where your Ki energy emanates from. Place both hands in an open flat position similar to a knife-hand, breath in deeply, and gradually raise both hands close together (palms facing upward) to the chin level, and then, at face level, press hands forward, keeping them together and exhaling. Place your hands so that your thumbs are spread and your fingertips nearly touch each other, and make a triangular shaped space between your fingers and hands. (Fig. 265, 266, 267)

Knees (Moo rup) are heavy weaponry that, when in range of a target, can deal a crippling blow against your opponent. You will never use them in competition, and there are only a few forms that incorporate their use. Knees are used for close combat because of their limited range. The power generated is from the largest muscle grouping in the body, incorporating the entire leg-torso-back-abdominal groups simultaneously. We strike with the front or top of the knee. Place your hand flat over your knee, with the fingers extended, and reach over the top of it so your fingertips just touch the bottom of your kneecap. The area that your hand is cupping is the area with which you should strike. (Fig. 268) Strike with either the front or top of the knee, aiming straight on to avoid damaging ligaments and tendons that surround the sides of the joint. Most knee strikes will include a hold or grab of your opponent, keeping them close for the attack and allowing you to further pull yourself into the strike. This will also give you greater balance because your opponent will probably have both feet on the ground when you execute the knee strike. The three points of ground contact (the opponent's two feet and your non-striking leg) creates, for a brief moment of time, stability like a tripod. Add force to your strike by snapping your pelvis upward and to the front at the same time the knee is snapped forward into the target. Knees can be used straight to the front, and diagonally into the ribs and torso like half of a roundhouse kick. Reset your feet for balance and preparedness for the next attack. Now, let's look at the specific targets for knee strikes.

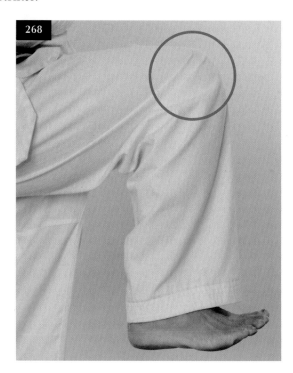

268

The **head** (Moo ree) is first grabbed with your two hands, which cup around the rear of the opponent's skull. Pull the head forward and down in front of you, while raising your knee directly into the head's downward motion. (Fig. 269, 270) This strike has a force like the head on collision between two cars. Because two forces collide, the consequence is a greatly magnified impact. Imagine two cars speeding towards each other going 50 mph. The actual collision speed is 100 mph, increasing the force of the impact. Pulling the head into the oncoming path of the knee creates the same exact type of magnified impact force. In training, carefully practice this technique as follows. When you grab your training partner's head, pull forward, but only with your two hands, letting them slide off the head. Don't actually pull the head; just let your hands slip around it, slapping them downward onto your raised knee. In this way you will not injure your partner's neck or face. Pantomime the execution to develop your range and timing, and to gain the experience that will ready you for defensive combat. Always remember to try your best to protect your partner and prevent training injuries.

The **stomach, torso and ribs** are wide open when two opponents grab each other's arms in a clinch. Even though we don't use a great deal of grappling in Tae Kwon Do (two Korean grappling styles are called Ssirium and Yudo), the reality is that the other guy may rely upon it. Using this close quarter technique allows you to reach your opponent's stomach and solar plexus with your knees. Set your feet firmly and balanced, with your knees bent, and while pulling or grasping your opponent, raise one knee into the midsection with speed and power. (Fig. 271) Repeat the strike if needed, and, if you're still in close quarters, follow up with elbows or fists. If your target has his ribs exposed when his arms are up, use your knee to strike to the lower ribs, as these are the most sensitive and vulnerable of all ribs. (Fig. 272) If you are in front, angle your kick as you might a roundhouse, and bring the knee across from the side at an angle. Strike repeatedly or as needed. Knee strikes to the chest, stomach and torso can be executed while standing to the side of an opponent if you pull them forward on an angle. They can also be executed without clinching. (Fig. 273)

The **groin** (Noolro) is probably the easiest target to reach with your knee because it's up front and at the right level. Move your knee and leg forward and up with power, perhaps even after cocking it by stepping to the rear slightly for a more exaggerated range of motion and increased power. (Fig. 274)

The **thighs** are the strongest part of our body, but not always the most protected. Leg attacks to the thighs can weaken and buckle them, and once your opponent is down, your escape or follow-up is easy. When fighting in close range, your knees are near your opponent's thighs. Knee strikes to the outer and inner thigh are practical. Either your kicks or your body positioning have to be at an angle from the centerline. When kneeing to the inside of the thigh, aim for the large central muscle group in the mid-center, or aim for the side of opponent's inner knee. When striking from the outside, you strike at mid-thigh to the rear of the midline. (Fig. 275) In this area, you will strike and shock the sciatic nerve and buckle the leg, possibly even breaking the femur. An enemy, who cannot walk, cannot chase and hurt you.

Elbow strikes are multi-directional close quarter weapons that transmit devastating power. There is no wrist to flex and no finger movement to reduce power. All power generated is transmitted directly to your target. Elbow (Pal goop) techniques are not as diverse as hands, but since they are hard weapons and maneuverable, they can produce heavy damage. The elbows can be thrown in all directions. The contact point of your strike is located just below the elbow on the front outer side of the forearm, or with the point of the elbow, depending on the circumstance of use. Secondary strikes can be added so the first strike is just one from a flurry. An example would be a right across hooking elbow to the face (Fig. 276), carried through, and immediately returned with a right hammer fist followed by a left hook, followed by a another right elbow back across again. That flurry produces four strikes in just over 1 second. Few people will still be standing after a blitz like that. For maximum power in elbow techniques, exaggerate your range of motions in practice. Put a lot of twist in your hips. Swivel your hips widely and turn your entire upper body, twisting your waist and reaching your shoulder fully across. You may also create a strike on the return back from your initial crossing strike. (Fig. 277) Practice these techniques on a heavy bag or striking bag to learn your reach, develop accuracy and expand your range of motion. The power of elbow strikes is often demonstrated at exhibitions with brick breaking or board breaking to illustrate the destructive power and impress audiences.

The basic maneuvers for elbow strikes are described below:

Front elbow uppercut starts with one of your hands pulled to the hip on the same side (in this example, the right hand is on the right hip). Aim with the elbow and arc forward and up, reaching your hand over your right shoulder to maximize the range of motion. Strike to the chin or body. To add power, raise your body into the strike, adding leg power. (Fig. 278)

A **cross elbow** starts with a hand positioned on the same side, coming up and across to the opposite side, much like a hook (in this example, the right hand moves from the right side to the left). Your target is the head or body. Twist your body into the technique to generate speed and power.

A **side striking elbow** is usually executed from a side stance rather than from the front. Using your elbow (in this example, your left) and attacking an opponent standing to your left side, enter a horse stance, or appropriate side stance variation. Fold by reaching your left hand to your right side, with the elbow close to your body. Step out to the left with your left foot while jabbing your elbow sharply to the left at your target. The striking arm can be supported by your other hand to generate more power by placing your right palm over the left fist, and striking with the combined force of both arms. Targets can be the opponent's face, chest, ribs, or any suitable opening that your opponent presents to you. Follow up as needed. (Fig. 279)

Elbows can be used as a finishing maneuver to end a conflict once and for all. A **down striking elbow** can break an enemy's spine, rupture a kidney or crush a skull. They are applied from a raised position similar to the end position of an uppercut. Begin with an elbow above your head, hand reached over the shoulder, and from there drop forward and down forcefully, by dropping your body weight and bending slightly at the waist, turning slightly so your elbow moves in to centerline. (Fig. 280) Use this technique after bending your opponent over with a front kick or a stomach, groin or solar plexus attack. These strikes will bend your opponent's body forward, creating an opportunity to follow up by dropping an elbow onto their back or neck when they present the target to you.

A **rear striking elbow** gives you defensive capability to places you can't always see. When an attacker attempts to grab you from the rear, a rearward directed elbow strike to the solar plexus, groin, ribs or throat will stop them in their tracks. (Fig. 281) To add another level of power, when striking with your elbow (in this example, it is the right elbow), make a fist with your right hand, and place your left hand over the front of the fist as support. When executing the strike, bring your right fist forward, cocking the elbow for an attack, and then with both hands together, slam it back into the opponent's body. Twist your body slightly adding hip power into the strike. You may drop very low and step out slightly, to better align your elbow with the opponent's target area. Or rise into the move for a high facial or neck attack, striking at your shoulder level.

TECHNIQUES

Tae Kwon Do has a large variety and assortment of **basic** kicks, punches and blocks that evolved over millennia. They are proven techniques that, when applied correctly, are extremely effective. They take time to learn and fully integrate into your useable arsenal. Learn your basics as well as you can. Watch everything your Grandmaster and instructors show you. Learn to mimic or copy every technique exactly as it is shown to you. Look at every little detail, and if you are unsure of a technique, ask someone for assistance and get coaching for your specific concern. If you do not learn each move properly, your foundation will be weak, and you may never attain your desired level of skill. Master the basics because everything that comes after is built upon that foundation. Like a house that needs a good foundation to support it throughout its lifetime, you also need a solid foundation upon which to build your Tae Kwon Do future.

Basic **techniques** in Tae Kwon Do follow a path of natural **progression** so that as one technique is learned, another can be taught that expands on what came before. You will start simply with some basic kicks, blocks and punches. You will learn to refine and perfect these techniques, learn when and why to use them, and then to add another move in sequence. You will learn to down block, and to combine that with a middle punch. Later you will add a kick. It's a building process that will take you on a journey from one belt level to the next, along with your accumulated knowledge and gradual advancement to more difficult movements.

Performing these basic practice combination techniques answers a question instructors get asked a lot by students. How can they tell what level a student is at, especially new students that may have training from another school? The answer is straight forward. Instructors can usually see precisely what level the student is because of their Tae Kwon Do skeleton. Their foundation of skills speaks for itself. If a person is only just competently executing front kicks and successfully executing blocks, we know they are still at the very beginning of their training, maybe no more than a month or two. But students competently executing a spinning back kick, yet still unable to smoothly and seamlessly add a move to that, might only be a yellow or green belt. As the skill level approaches black belt, it becomes harder to exactly pinpoint the belt level. But there's usually no mistaking an experienced black belt.

Combinations are movements that use two or more kicks, punches and blocks in an order that assures your movements are flowing and effective. Combination techniques are more effective than one punch moves or individual kicks. They provide a one-two-three punch or kick punch that is triple the attack of an individual move. String these techniques together and you have non-stop attacks that place your opponent on the defensive, and give you the advantage. In theory, the one punch takeout is ideal, but in reality, you will likely need an effective combination or "flurry" to do the job right. The combination may start with a defensive block and a counterattack with a double stepping front kick to drive your opponent back. As you progress in your training, you will add a greater variety of kicks and punches, even attacking and defending to different directions. Poomse, or forms, are an example of sequential combinations of moves. They may have from 20 to 40 individual movements combined in a single flowing pattern to represent specific fighting scenarios. Forms are miniature hand-to-hand battles against unseen opponents that we practice over and over so we can automatically execute these techniques when the need arises. As we progress in Tae Kwon Do, these forms become more complex and add new movements to expand our choices. And as our skill and understanding continue to grow, our flexibility and choices of techniques do as well.

There is a **progression** to the punching and kicking in Tae Kwon Do that naturally allows you to increase the variety and improve the way that you apply your combinations. Most any movement can be executed from a stationary position, say from a back stance. We can even stand in that one position and flurry with our chosen combination. We kick with our lead legs, or our rear legs. We switch feet and kick with either leg. But because we are continually moving in a real situation (moving targets are harder to hit than stationary targets) we add different types of movements like steps and skips to expand the choices, to close distances quickly or otherwise surprise our opponent.

Stepping kicks are the first stage of movement and can be applied to all kicks. Begin in fighting stance (in this example, with the left foot back). Step the left foot forward, front kick with the rear (right) leg, set the foot down to the front, step forward with your left foot once again, and kick again with the right leg a second time. (Fig. 001, 002, 003, 004, 005, 006) For full weapon development, follow each kick with a lead hand high punch. Practice this to both directions and with the left and right legs and hands.

Next, we add a **sliding** (Mikulgi chagie) step to the kick. Start in fighting stance. Slide the rear (left) foot forward and next to the front foot to close up your stance, and immediately kick with the front leg. Repeat for consecutive kicks. These are short explosive kicks that drive a person back, and you are closing the distance and continuing your attack as they retreat. (Fig. 007, 008, 009, 010)

Skipping techniques require lightness on your feet, and produce extra reach when closing the distance to your opponent. Start in fighting stance (in this example, left foot is back). Bring your rear (left) foot up and past your front foot, holding it off the ground and then kicking with your right foot. This differs from a sliding technique in that the rear foot is drawn off the ground, and past the front foot so fast that the kick is executed at the same time as the skipping rear foot is being set down. (Fig. 011, 012, 013, 014)

Spinning kick (Dolmyo chagie) techniques are of mid-level difficulty that add a second, or reversing, direction to your techniques. You can use them with roundhouse, wheel, hook, side, axe and twist kicks.

Starting in fighting stance (in this example, the right foot is back) (Fig. 015), look to the rear over your right shoulder, while turning your front (left) foot 180° to the rear. (Fig. 016) Bend your left knee and take the bulk of your weight onto the ball of your left foot. While continuing your turning motion to the rear, raise your right leg (Fig. 017) and execute the

hook kick as described previously (Fig. 018, 019), swinging it fully around after striking the target to land in its original position to your rear. (Fig. 020, 021) Your foot will travel in a 360° arc, extending out and striking the target. A back sidekick will be executed in a similar way, except that the kick is in a straight line to the front, and the return motion is continued straight back to land where it started at the rear after traveling 360°.

Once you get comfortable with spinning techniques, build on them; try the kick with a step forward. This then is a step spinning move that can close distance and confuse your opponent as to where the actual kick will finally come from.

Jumping kicking (Ddweyo chagie) techniques are executed by jumping off the ground, having scissored off the opposite leg. Putting your entire body weight into the technique helps in magnifying the power. Start in fighting stance (in this example, with the left foot back). (Fig. 022) We will kick with the front (right) leg. Raise the rear leg as though moving forward. (Fig. 023) While this leg is still raised high off the ground, switch or scissor your legs across each other, executing the kick with the right leg. (Fig. 024, 025, 026, 027) Land on the left leg, placing your kicking right leg again to the front in fighting stance. Start practicing this with small jumps. Distance and height will develop over time.

Jump spinning kicks are at the highest level in the progression. They are exactly as they sound, with the jumping and rotational aspects of both kicks incorporated into the single move. It requires speed and agility and not just a little bit of acrobatics. These techniques are most frequently used in competition events or Tae Kwon Do exhibitions. They continue to increase in difficulty with multiple rotations, such as the 540° jump spinning roundhouse kick and 720° jump spinning hook. Although there are limits to what the human body can realistically do, there are some techniques so difficult that there are only a few individuals that can actually perform them. At upcoming exhibitions of Tae Kwon Do around the world, we can expect to see ever more impressive and difficult techniques performed

for their entertainment value. As Tae Kwon Do continues to grow, and practitioners practice original and unusual demonstration techniques, we will see maneuvers in the future that, as of now, few of us might even imagine. (Fig. 028)

ONE STEP SPARRING (Han bun gyroogi)

Up to now, we've learned how to use our hands, our feet and the blocks that will protect us. We've built on a foundation of basics and learned how these techniques work. Now we must practice them to perfection so that, should we ever need to use a technique, it will be fast powerful and effective.

One-step sparring techniques are taught with basic techniques from the yellow belt progressing in greater complexity and diversity of technique all the way to black belt. This is how we begin learning to defend ourselves against potential real life dangers, sharpen and improve our timing, range, and reflexes, and develop our overall control. One-steps are a short series of blocks, kicks and punches in response to a single attacking move. These are pre-arranged "skirmishes" that provide the skill and experience to learn what works, and what doesn't. You will gradually learn to create your own one-step sparring techniques, and the experience of this practice will guide you in using what is useful and, more specifically, what works for you. We usually prepare the scenario with our partner attacking while we defend against it.

One-steps follow a specific procedure and starting sequence so nobody ever gets hurt. Start by facing each other at attention, and bow. Jhoom-be. Your partner, as the attacker, steps the right foot back, entering into a left front stance, while the left hand down blocks. You, as the defender, enter into a mirror image of that stance, also known as open stance (Fig. 029), stepping the left foot back, entering into a right front stance, while the right hand down blocks. Stepping back assures you maintain your distance from each other for the exercise. You will both Keeyup together, at the same time, when stepping back into your respective front stances. The attacker may then immediately attack, stepping forward into front stance with his right foot, and executing a right fist middle or high punch with a Keeyup. You will now respond with your pre-planned defense. Please note that as you progress through the belt levels, your defending stance may vary with the different one-step defenses in either an open or closed stance. A closed stance is if you both step back with the same leg (either both with the right leg or both with the left leg), which really looks like an opposite sided stance, not a mirror image stance. (Fig. 030) For example, from the open stance, your (the defender's) left foot steps forward and to your left, blocking the attacker's punch with a right hand outer block, followed by a double punch to the ribs. Keeyup. When finished, return to Jhoom-be stance, bow, and resume the exercise. Practice each technique several times to each side, then switch roles with your attacker so he or she may practice defense.

Timing, as mentioned earlier, is critical to your success. Start your defense too late and you've allowed your attacker to penetrate your defense and you will likely get hit or over-run. Respond too soon and you may allow your attacker an advantageous opportunity for a change of tactic. Wait, while remaining alert to the actual movements of your attacker. Time your defense for greatest effectiveness. Practice is your best guide for acquiring this learning experience. With one-steps, you already know what's coming, so wait and "see" the movement. Watch your opponent for every little movement. Keep your eyes centrally focused so you can see his or her feet and face. Be alert to movements the opponent may make that gives away their intent, known as "telegraphing". An example of "telegraphing" is someone who may cock or draw back the attacking hand slightly before punching. Be alert for giveaway tips that you can exploit. And be aware of your own little telegraphing movements. We must first become aware that we too may be doing this, and identify what it is before we can discipline ourselves to stop. In real situations and competitions, numerous feints and false movements are incorporated into the sparring as invitations to a set-up, drawing the opponent into a pre-arranged plan of attack. These feints are made to entice you to enter the web of your opponent. Stay aware and alert. And stick to your basics.

We will explore 25 one-step techniques starting with beginning techniques and progressing to black belt one-steps. These examples are representative of commonly taught practical one-steps. There are schools that use two or three techniques for each belt level. There are schools that encourage you to create your own. Try both, in that order. Learn what your Grandmaster and Instructors present to you and practice it to perfection, and then experiment with similar derivations, not wildly different ones. For example, if you chose a front kick for a technique, substituting it for the sidekick you were shown, you will soon discover that it may not work due to lack of reach, or it may present the front of your body where it would get you trashed. This is all a part of your creative, open-minded learning process. Be open to everything you are shown and taught. Don't reject suggestions from seniors and instructors. As one large Tae Kwon Do family, we are here for the same reasons, and we are a sister and brotherhood. We have often heard the expression "each one teach one" over the course of our training, and it is a good philosophy to adopt. This is another way that knowledge is shared and passed on to others.

Start with the attacker in front stance, right leg back, left hand down block. Attacker steps forward into a right front stance, and executes a right middle or high punch. Defender starts in open stance, or closed stance as specified. Keeyup loudly after each one-step is complete, or on each striking move.

1) **Defense against middle punch.** *Open stance.* (1A) Step left foot to front stance, left hand outer middle block (1B), right hand middle punch. Keeyup. (1C)

2) **Defense against high punch.** *Open stance.* (2A) Step left foot to front stance, left hand high (rising) block, right hand high punch. Keeyup. (2B)

3) **Defense against high punch.** *Closed stance.* (3A) Step right foot into front stance, right hand high (rising) block, left hand punch to armpit. Keeyup. (3B)

4) **Defense against middle punch.** *Open stance.* (4A) Left foot steps forward into back stance, left hand outer middle block. (4B) Then, shift left foot forward into front stance and execute left hand knife-hand block. (4C) Follow with right hand middle punch. Keeyup. (4D)

5) **Defense against middle punch.** *Open stance.* (5A) Side step left foot 45° forward and to the outside into horse riding stance, left hand inner middle knife-hand block. (5B) Follow with two middle punches (5C) (right hand and then left) (5D), and finish with right hand high punch. Keeyup.

6) **Defense against high punch.** *Open stance.* (6A) Left foot steps forward into horse riding stance, left hand armpit attack. Keeyup. (6B)

7) **Defense against middle punch.** *Open stance.* (7A) Left leg executes inside to outside crescent (wheel) kick (7B), then right leg front kick to midsection. Keeyup. (7C)

8) **Defense against middle punch.** *Closed stance.* (8A) Right leg executes inside to outside crescent (wheel) kick. (8B) Then execute left leg roundhouse kick to ribs. Keeyup. (8C)

9) **Defense against high punch.** *Open stance.* (9A) Step forward to left front stance, execute left high (rising) block while at the same time executing right high punch. Keeyup. (9B)

10) **Defense against middle punch.** *Closed stance.* (10A) Right leg slides forward 45° angle to the right (side step) to fighting stance. Left leg roundhouse to face (or solar plexus). Keeyup. (10B)

11) **Defense against middle punch.** *Closed stance.* (11A) Right foot steps forward to natural stance and pivots off the ball of the right foot, turning into a side facing stance and executing right hand push (palm) block. (11B) The same hand grabs opponent's wrist, execute stationary right leg side kick. Keeyup. (11C)

12) **Defense against high punch.** *Open stance.* (12A) Left leg side kick (12B), followed by right leg roundhouse kick to face. Left leg returns to a position beside, but forward of, the right leg, allowing for effective range for roundhouse kick. Keeyup. (12C)

13) **Defense against high punch.** *Open stance.* (13A) Left foot steps forward into horse riding stance, left hand executes an armpit attack. (13B) Then move left foot out to front stance and execute left knife-hand block followed by right high punch. Keeyup. (13C)

14) **Defense against high punch.** *Closed stance.* (14A) Right foot steps forward into front stance, while left knee drops almost to the ground executing right hand low punch to groin. (14B) Then move left foot into a long right walking stance and execute a left middle punch. (14C) Follow by sliding left leg in a bit more into a short stance and right hand high punch. Keeyup. (14D)

15) **Defense against high punch.** *Open stance.* (15A) Left foot moves forward to front stance and execute left rising (high) knife-hand block. (15B) Follow with right hand neck attack. Keeyup. (15C, 15D)

16) **Defense against middle punch.** *Closed stance.* (16A) Right foot steps forward and to the outside into back stance while executing right hand double knife-hand block. (16B) Right hand grabs and twists opponent's wrist, then left foot side-steps (16C) followed by right leg roundhouse kick. Keeyup. (16D)

17) **Defense against high punch.** *Closed stance.* (17A) Step right foot
   forward to right front stance, execute left outer knife-hand block
   and simultaneous right hand neck attack. (17B) Then, pull right leg
   back into natural stance grabbing attacker's wrist. (17C) Wrist grab
   (inset), and execute right hand reverse neck attack. Keeyup. (17D)

18) **Defense against middle punch.** *Closed stance.* (18A) Right leg executes outside to inside crescent kick (18B), then left leg spinning back kick. Keeyup. (18C)

19) **Defense against high punch.** *Closed stance.* (19A) Right leg front kicks to groin (19B), then left leg front kick to armpit. Keeyup. (19C)

20) **Defense against middle punch.** *Open stance.* (20A) Left leg side steps into horse riding stance, left hand executes inner knife-hand block. (20B) Follow with double middle punch to body (20C), (right hand then left). (20D) Then, chamber left hand to hip and right hand to left side of your neck (as preparing for knife-hand block) ready to grab opponent's wrist. (20E) At the same time, execute high left hand punch and grab opponent's wrist from the outside (20F), twisting your body and pulling him or her forward and down, and then execute a right leg roundhouse kick to his or her face. Keeyup. (20G)

21) **Defense against middle punch.** *Open stance.* (21A) Step left foot
into back stance and execute left outer middle block. (21B) From
back stance, execute left foot step slide into left front stance, executing a right hand middle punch. Keep left guarding hand up
during the transition and punch. Keeyup. (21C)

22) **Defense against middle punch.** *Open stance.* (22A) Left foot side steps, and then execute a right leg push kick to back of knee. (22B) Next, execute a left leg spinning wheel or spinning hook kick. Keeyup. (22C)

23) **Defense against middle punch.** *Closed stance.* (23A) Step right foot forward into right back stance, execute right hand inner middle block. (23B) Then, turn to the left, stepping into cat stance, and execute a left elbow attack to mid-section (the left elbow can be supported with the right hand for greater power), (23C), followed by left back-fist to face. Keeyup. (23D)

24) **Defense against middle punch.** *Closed stance.* (24A) Step right foot forward into back stance, and execute right hand inner middle block. (24B) Then execute sliding right elbow attack in horse stance. (24C) Move right foot into front stance and execute right high back fist (24D), followed by left middle punch. Keeyup. (24E)

25) **Defense against high punch.** *Open stance.* (25A) Step left foot to outside in front stance executing left high (rising) block. (25B) Right foot steps through while executing right elbow to ribs. (25C) Then, without stepping, twist left, to the rear, and execute a left elbow attack to the ribs, right hand supported. Keeyup. (25D)

Three-step sparring (Sae bun gyroogi) has similarities to one-steps, but are extended for realism and advanced learning. Three steps begin the exact same way as one-steps. The difference is that you are attacked by three punches moving towards you. Counter each while moving to your rear until the third punch is thrown. Then, after the last block, counter-attack your opponent, as you would with your one-steps.

For example: Jhoom-be. Opponent attacks with right punch. From a closed stance, left leg forward, you step the left leg rear into back stance, right hand inside knife-hand block. For the second punch (opponent's left hand), step right foot to rear in back stance, left hand knife-hand blocks. For the third punch (opponent's right hand) step left foot to rear into back stance, right knife-hand block. Immediately, lead leg (right) side kicks to mid-section, landing in horse stance, executing triple punch to mid-section, grabbing head and pulling down, smashing face with knee.

There are an endless variety of combinations to use for three-steps, as you have learned. Practice these and perfect them. Learn what works, what is most simple and effective for your body type, and what comes naturally to you.

There may be a time in your life when you find yourself in a situation where you are attacked when sitting on a chair or a couch, from a kneeling position, or even lying on the ground. The techniques you are learning can be applied, within limits, in many situations. Front kicks can be executed while sitting in a chair. Sidekicks can be executed from the ground at an opponent reaching down at you. Blocks, likewise, can be executed to deflect an attack and create the opportunity to regain your footing or balance. Think freely, and let your techniques flow in response to the attacks. You will discover that your abilities will continue to progress with regular practice.

POOMSE, HYUNG, PATTERNS OR FORMS

Tae Kwon Do forms are a series of simulated attacks and blocks practiced to different directions in a pre-arranged pattern. There are different Poomse, also called Hyung (Kata is the Japanese term), for different belt levels, progressing in complexity with new moves added level by level. Each Poomse has a different meaning, but as a whole they symbolize the various phenomena of planet Earth. These include what are referred to in the "Palgwe" Poomse (patterns) as "The eight powers of the Universe", which are Heaven, Joyfulness, Fire, Thunder, Wind, Water, Mountains and Earth. The symbolism of the Taeguek Hyung are essentially the same.

Patterns allow us to practice what we are taught, and to see how the offensive and defensive techniques are applied. We practice a different form at every belt level, and will continue to practice our first forms along with our newer forms throughout our Tae Kwon Do career. Each form adds stances, blocks or kicks, a few at a time until we have much of what we learned incorporated into patterns at the higher belt levels. Poomse are practiced individually, with a partner, or in a group. There are just too many possible kicking and punching combinations for the Poomse to contain everything, so not everything is in all pattern sets. For example, there are no roundhouse kicks in the Palgwe forms. Forms don't show everything that's possible. Where one specific strike is suitable, substituting another kick or punch might be as effective. So even if a form does not contain every possible individual strike, it has little impact on the practical intent of the application. In a real fight, you will keep kicks basic, low and fast.

There are different ways of performing Poomse with each style offering something new, such as balance, speed, or awareness. There are some standard guidelines you should know when working on Poomse; first, start and end at the same spot; second, maintain the correct stances and posture at all times, being both relaxed and snappy with your technique; third, perform every movement completely and smoothly, and in accordance to the tempo and power of the pattern as you are taught; and fourth, Keeyup loudly when appropriate to shout.

Poomse can be practiced with elements from every style, and do not necessarily have to be performed in only a single style. Some elements of the different styles are mixed in throughout the entire set of patterns. The various styles of execution include the following:

Regular style is performed with rapid, sharp and crisp movements throughout, pausing only long enough between moves to show they are distinct from each other.

Fast motion style is performed at an accelerated speed, while retaining elements of smoothness and accuracy of technique.

Slow motion is executed in a slower than normal speed, concentrating on perfect technique, balance and full range of motion for every move.

Concentration style is executed with intense power completely and smoothly throughout the technique, ending in a sharp and abrupt end to each movement.

Ballet style is a soft, graceful, flowing performance that emphasizes the beauty of Tae Kwon Do.

Blindfolded Poomse promote visualization requiring you to see each movement and your position in the Dojang in your mind. It improves balance, sense of direction, confidence, and lets you know if your natural spacing for stances needs adjusting based upon where you end your Poomse. Even blindfolded, you should end where you begin.

Musical Poomse are performed to a piece of music that has a tempo or beat that corresponds to your form. Moves are executed in time with the music for a dramatic presentation.

Creative Poomse are patterns of your own design or choosing, sometimes with music, that you perform at tournaments. Most competitors choose patterns that emphasize their strengths and show their abilities to the maximum.

Many Masters believe that Poomse are at the heart of Tae Kwon Do. Poomse seem to be very different from other Tae Kwon Do techniques and applications, especially modern sparring. But these Masters respond that, "Without Poomse, there can be no Tae Kwon Do". Poomse gives you the ability to practice on your own and in any location. And the more you practice, and the older you get, the more you will appreciate their beauty and applications. Poomse become a moving meditation because your mind and body are working as one for a single purpose. You become focused, and your entire being is set to the immediate task of the performance of each individual move. Practice them to perfection. As you progress through the belt levels and learn another Poomse, and then another, do the following: When you practice, start with the first Poomse you ever learned, and then move to the next one, performing each one in order until you are at your current Poomse. Feel free to practice the new form as needed, but by keeping the practice up, you strengthen your foundation and make your knowledge permanent.

THE FORMS

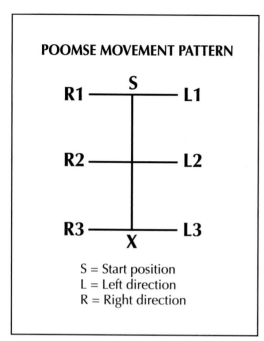

POOMSE MOVEMENT PATTERN

S = Start position
L = Left direction
R = Right direction

As a white belt you will be taught a form, or several forms, for beginners. It may contain nothing but blocks and punches. This is part of what new students learn during their first few weeks of training. Patterns follow a pre-arranged design. Most lower belt Tae Kwon Do patterns follow the lines of the uppercase letter "I"; or an uppercase "H" lying on its side. Take a look at the pattern chart. You start in the back (top center of the chart), facing the front, (bottom of the chart). The moves turn left and right and around, but you follow this pattern as if it were drawn on the floor. As the forms get more complex there are angles and cross lines to the main "I" pattern. Some forms at higher levels just go straight up and back, or only from side to side. The Taegeuk poomse follow a pattern representing and similar in design to the "gwe" symbols, with three cross bars and an imaginary center line running through and connecting them.

When performing the Taegeuk poomse, your movements will follow the pattern shown above for all 8 forms. "S" is your starting and ending position. With each Poomse, you will begin at this position, facing "X" which is at the far end or opposite side of the pattern. "L" means the direction to your left from the starting position, and "R" means the direction to your right from the starting position. When you have reached the "X" position, and begin movements back to "S" once again, your real left and right will be reversed, but for the sake of clarity, we will continue to use the L1, L2 or L3 or R1, R2, and R3 movement directions to eliminate confusion. This will be described in each poomse as your guide.

THE TAEGEUK HYUNG

Taegeuk Poomse are designed in accordance with the Taegeuk principles of Um-Yang, the opposing phenomena or forces of nature. This principle is called Yin-Yang in Chinese. It is the interaction of these two forces, which created all things and encompasses the vastness of the universe. Taegeuk therefore has no pre-defined form, no beginning, and no ending. The symbol of Um-Yang is a circle with an "S" shaped line through the middle, which overlaps both halves, equally.

Understand that the symbol is not just a circle divided into two halves. Both halves interact to form different degrees of Um and Yang, but as a whole the opposing forces are equal. In order for one to exist, the opposite must also exist. Night and day. Heaven and Earth. Right and wrong. Love and hate. Good and evil. Life and death. Hard and soft. Attack and retreat. Offense and defense. All things co-exist and one must learn to create a harmonious balance to develop the ultimate good.

Taegeuk Poomse are considered the moderns forms, and emphasize the walking stance, and the more modern movements of Tae Kwon Do. In this book we illustrate only the Taegeuk patterns, because they are the official forms of the World Taekwondo Federation (WTF) and are most familiar to Tae Kwon Do students at the present time. Many schools still teach the Palgwe's, and some teach them only as a second set of patterns upon becoming a black belt, to better balance your knowledge and skills. The ideal would be to also show the Palgwe in this book, because the original design in creating the Taegeuk was for their complementary nature. The Um-Yang has an equal yet opposite side to everything in life, and illustrates the natural balance of all things. In forms, the softer (Um) style of the Taegeuk are opposite but complementary to the Palgwe's harder (Yang) style. Taegeuk are like the flowing movement and liquidity of the oceans, as opposed to the solidity and firmness of the mountains as represented in the Palgwe.

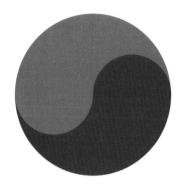

These forms as presented are the current accepted patterns for the WTF and Kukkiwon. This is now important because in September 2006 the First World Poomse Championships will have taken place. The judging takes into consideration the accuracy of Poomse performance in accordance with the new unified patterns, along with style and presentation. Please be aware that several of the movements in these forms may differ slightly from what is taught at your school. This is simply because many Grandmasters have in some cases made several small adjustments to better balance the Poomse. In other cases, these differences were how your Grandmaster was originally taught many decades ago. It is common for high belt practitioners to still practice the way they were taught, even though there are now "official" forms recognized for competition. The few differences are minor and often serve to strengthen the form as a whole.

STARTING A POOMSE

Each time you start a Poomse, be specific in your approach. This is very straight forward at the Dojang; but in the competition ring it is somewhat more formal and elaborate, with names and sometimes rank stated. In the Dojang though, you approach the start position when asked or called upon by your instructor. Immediately stand at attention (Charyeot), even if you are not explicitly told to do so. Usually, you will be facing your Grandmaster or instructor. Bow (Kyung neh). Clearly state the name of your Poomse. "Poomse Taegeuk Il Jang", for example. Your instructor will say Jhoom-be, which means to enter "ready stance". Next you will be instructed "Si-jack", which means to begin. Start your Poomse, and upon completion, hold your last move without moving or looking around. Wait until you hear "Bahrote", which means to finish or return, called out, and return to the ready position (Jhoom-be"). Next you will hear "Sho", which means to relax. Return to attention and bow. Additional instructions will be given to you at this time, or you will be dismissed. Always bow, and take a step back before exiting the training floor.

During the performance of the Poomse, you might be moving as part of a group, or by yourself. Often your instructor will call out the number of the move, and you will make your move in response. At other times, such as during testing, you may be instructed to do it "by yourself, no count" which means you begin and move from start to finish on your own and without an auditory count. Keep a steady tempo to your moves, and perform them with confidence. When performing with other students as a group, stay together so that you appear to move simultaneously, as a single entity.

Taegeuk Il Jang (1 jang), 8th Gup

This Poomse is represented by the trigram "Keon" (comprised of three solid bars), which means heaven and yang. Taegeuk Il Jang symbolizes the beginning of the creation of all things in the universe, as does this Poomse in the training of Tae Kwon Do, by presenting the most basic techniques.

Charyeot. (Fig. A) Kyung neh. (Fig. B) Poomse Taegeuk Il Jang. Jhoom-be. (Fig. C) Si-jack!

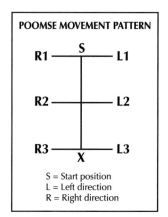

POOMSE MOVEMENT PATTERN

R1 —— S —— L1

R2 ————— L2

R3 —— X —— L3

S = Start position
L = Left direction
R = Right direction

1) Look left, step left foot 90° (facing L1) to left walking stance, left hand down block.

2) Step right foot forward to right walking stance, right hand middle punch.

3) Look over right shoulder. Step your right foot 180° to your rear (facing R1) turning on the ball of your left foot into right walking stance, right hand down block.

4) Left foot steps forward into left walking stance, left hand middle punch.

Taegeuk Il Jang (1 jang)

5) Look left, stepping left foot 90° to your left (facing X) into left front stance, left hand down block.

6) Without stepping, right hand reverse middle punch.

7) Swivel 90° to the right on the ball of your left foot (facing R2), pulling right foot towards you into right walking stance, left hand inner middle block.

8) Step left foot forward into left walking stance, right hand reverse middle punch.

9) Look over your left shoulder. Step your left foot 180° to the rear (facing L2), turning on the ball of your right foot, stepping into left walking stance, right hand inner middle block.

10) Right foot steps forward into right walking stance, left hand middle reverse punch.

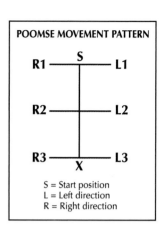

POOMSE MOVEMENT PATTERN

S = Start position
L = Left direction
R = Right direction

Taegeuk Il Jang (1 jang)

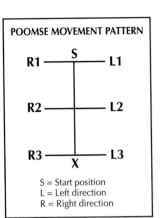

POOMSE MOVEMENT PATTERN

R1 —— S —— L1

R2 ———— L2

R3 —— X —— L3

S = Start position
L = Left direction
R = Right direction

11) Step right foot 90° to the right (facing X) turning on the ball of your left foot, stepping into right front stance, right hand down block.

12) Without stepping, left hand reverse middle punch.

13) Step left foot 90° to the left (facing L3), into left walking stance left hand rising block.

14A) Right (rear) leg front kick,

14B) landing to front in right walking stance, right hand middle punch.

Taegeuk Il Jang (1 jang)

15) Right foot steps 180° to the rear (facing R3), turning on the ball of your left foot, landing in right walking stance, right hand rising block.

16A) Left (rear) leg front kick

16B) landing to the front in left walking stance, left hand middle punch.

Taegeuk Il Jang (1 jang)

17) Left foot steps 90° to the right (facing S), turning on the ball of the right foot, into left front stance, left hand down block.

18) Right foot steps forward into right front stance, right hand middle punch. **Keeyup!**

Bahrote. (Fig. D) Turn on the ball of the right foot 180° to the left, returning to starting position (facing X). End in ready stance. Sho. Return to attention by bringing left foot to the right foot, and bow. (Fig. E)

Taegeuk Ee Jang (2 jang), 7th Gup

This Poomse is represented by the trigram "Tae" (comprised of one broken upper bar and two solid lower bars), which signifies inner firmness and outer softness.

Charyeot. Kyung neh. Poomse Taegeuk Ee Jang. Jhoom-be. Si-jack!

1) Look left. Step left foot 90° (facing L1) forward into left walking stance, left hand down block.

2) Step right foot forward into right front stance, right hand middle punch.

3) Step right foot 180° to the rear (facing R1), turning on the ball of your left foot, landing in right walking stance, right hand down block.

4) Step left foot forward into left front stance, left hand middle punch.

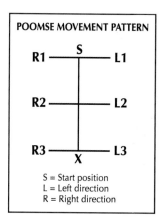

POOMSE MOVEMENT PATTERN

R1 —— S —— L1

R2 —————— L2

R3 —— X —— L3

S = Start position
L = Left direction
R = Right direction

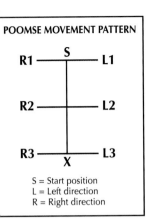

POOMSE MOVEMENT PATTERN

```
R1 ——— S ——— L1
        |
R2 ——— | ——— L2
        |
R3 ——— X ——— L3
```

S = Start position
L = Left direction
R = Right direction

5) Turn left foot 90° to the left (facing X), on ball of right foot, stepping left foot in front into left walking stance, right hand inner middle block.

6) Right foot steps forward into right walking stance, left hand inner middle block.

7) Turn 90° to the left (facing L2) on ball of the right foot, stepping into left walking stance, left hand down block.

8A) Right foot front kicks,

8B) landing forward in right front stance, right hand high punch.

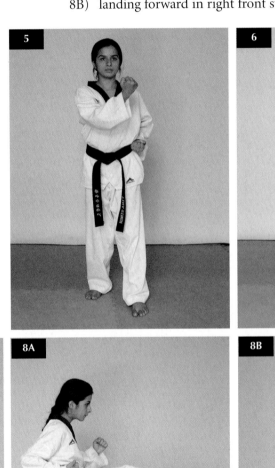

Taegeuk Ee Jang (2 jang)

9) Turn to the right, step right foot 180° to the rear (facing R2) on ball of left foot, stepping to right walking stance, right hand low block.

10A) Left foot front kick,

10B) landing forward in left front stance, left hand high punch.

11) Turn 90° to the left (facing X) on the ball of your right foot to left walking stance, left hand rising block.

12) Step right foot forward to right walking stance, right hand rising block.

13) Look over your left shoulder. Turn 270° to your left on ball of right foot (facing R3), turning to your rear by bringing left foot around behind to your left and landing in left walking stance, right hand inner middle block.

14) Look right. Step right foot 180° to the rear (facing L3) turning on ball of left foot, landing in right walking stance, left inner middle block.

15) Step left foot 90° to the left (facing S) turning on the ball of the right foot, landing in left walking stance, left hand down block.

16A) Right foot front kick,

16B) landing front in right walking stance, right hand middle punch.

Taegeuk Ee Jang (2 jang)

17A) Left foot front kick,

17B) landing front in left walking stance, left hand middle punch.

18A) Right foot front kick,

18B) landing front in right walking stance, right hand middle punch. **Keeyup!**

Bahrote. Turn 180° to the left (facing X) on the ball of your right foot, bringing your left foot back to starting position and facing front. Sho. Return to attention. Kyung neh. Bow.

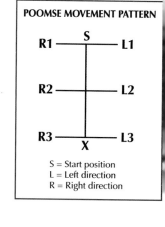

POOMSE MOVEMENT PATTERN

S = Start position
L = Left direction
R = Right direction

Taegeuk Ee Jang (2 jang)

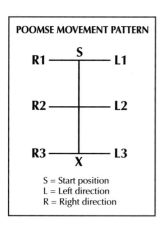
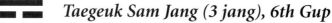

Taegeuk Sam Jang (3 jang), 6th Gup

This Poomse is represented by the trigram "Ri" (comprised of a solid upper and lower bar and a broken middle bar), which means "hot and bright", or fire.

Charyeot. Kyung Neh. Poomse Taegeuk Sam Jang. Jhoom-be. Si-jack!

1) Look left. Turn and step left foot 90° to the left (facing L1) into left walking stance, left hand down block.

2A) Right foot front kick,

2B) landing forward in right front stance, right hand middle punch,

2C) immediately followed by a reverse left hand middle punch without stepping.

Taegeuk Sam Jang (3 jang)

3) Look over right shoulder. Step right foot 180° to the rear (facing R1) pivoting on the ball of your left foot, and landing in right walking stance, right hand down block.

4A) Left foot front kick,

4B) landing to front in left front stance, left hand middle punch,

4C) immediately followed by a reverse right hand middle punch without stepping.

5) Look left, and step left foot 90° to the left (facing X), turning on the ball of right foot, stepping left foot into left walking stance, right knife-hand strike to the neck.

6) Step right foot forward into right walking stance, left knife-hand strike to the neck.

7) Fixing right foot, step left foot 90° to left (facing L2) into left foot forward back stance, left hand single knife-hand middle block.

8) With right foot fixed, slide left foot into left front stance, right hand reverse middle punch.

9) Look over right shoulder. Turn 180° to the rear on the ball of the left foot (facing R2), stepping right foot into right foot forward back stance, right hand single knife-hand middle block.

10) Keeping left foot fixed in place, slide right foot into right front stance, left hand reverse middle punch.

Taegeuk Sam Jang (3 jang)

11) Turn 90° to the left (facing X) on the ball of your right foot, stepping into left walking stance, right inner middle block.

12) Step right foot forward into right walking stance, left hand inner middle block.

13) Look left. Turn left 270° to the rear (facing R3) on the ball of the right foot, into a left walking stance, left hand down block.

14A) Right foot front kick,

14B) landing forward in right front stance, right hand middle punch,

14C) immediately followed by a left hand reverse middle punch without stepping.

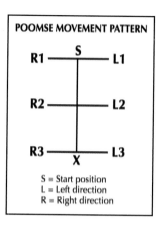

POOMSE MOVEMENT PATTERN

R1 —— S —— L1

R2 —————— L2

R3 —— X —— L3

S = Start position
L = Left direction
R = Right direction

Taegeuk Sam Jang (3 jang)

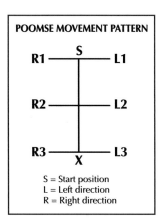

POOMSE MOVEMENT PATTERN

S = Start position
L = Left direction
R = Right direction

15) Look over right shoulder. Turn 180° to the right (facing L3) on the ball of the left foot, landing in right walking stance, right hand down block.

16A) Left foot front kick,

16B) landing forward in left front stance, left hand middle punch,

16C) immediately followed by a right hand reverse middle punch without stepping.

Taegeuk Sam Jang (3 jang)

17A) Turn 90° to the left (facing S) on the ball of the right foot, stepping into left walking stance, left hand down block,

17B) immediately followed by a right hand reverse middle punch without stepping.

18A) Step right foot forward into right walking stance, right hand down block,

18B) immediately followed by a left reverse middle punch without stepping.

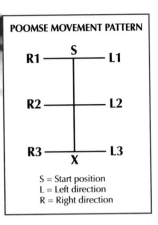

POOMSE MOVEMENT PATTERN

```
R1 ——— S ——— L1


R2 ——————— L2


R3 ——— X ——— L3
```

S = Start position
L = Left direction
R = Right direction

19A) Left foot front kick,

19B) landing forward in left walking stance, left hand low block,

19C) immediately followed by a right hand reverse middle punch without stepping.

Taegeuk Sam Jang (3 jang)

20A) Right foot front kick,

20B) landing forward in right walking stance, right hand down block,

20C) immediately followed by a left hand reverse middle punch without stepping. **Keeyup!**

Bahrote. Turn 180° to the left (the rear) on the ball of your right foot (facing X) to start position. Sho. Bow.

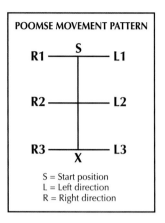

POOMSE MOVEMENT PATTERN

R1 — S — L1

R2 — L2

R3 — X — L3

S = Start position
L = Left direction
R = Right direction

Taegeuk Sa Jang (4 jang), 5th Gup

This Poomse is represented by the trigram "Jin" (comprised of a broken top and middle bar and a solid lower bar), which represents thunder, and great power and dignity.

Charyeot. Kyung neh. Poomse Taegeuk Sa Jang. Jhoom-be. Si-jack!

1) Look left. Step left foot 90° to the left (facing L1) into left foot forward back stance, double knife-hand middle block.

2) Step right foot forward into right front stance, executing right hand assisted spear-hand thrust to solar plexus.

3) Look right. Step right foot back 180° turning (facing R1) on the ball of the left foot, entering into right foot forward back stance, double knife-hand middle block.

4) Step left foot forward into left front stance, executing left hand assisted spear-hand thrust to solar plexus.

Taegeuk Sa Jang (4 jang)

5) Step left foot 90° to the left (facing X) turning on ball of the right foot, stepping into left front stance, executing right swallow form knife-hand strike.

6A) Right foot (rear leg) front kick.

6B) landing with foot forward in right front stance, left hand reverse middle punch.

7) Left foot (rear) sidekick, landing to front in left front stance.

8A) Right leg (rear) sidekick,

8B) landing to front in right foot forward back stance, double knife-hand middle block.

9) Look left. Turn 270° to the left (facing R3) on ball of right foot, stepping into left foot forward back stance, left hand outer middle block (palm of fist facing front).

10A) Right leg (rear leg) front kick,

10B) returning foot to original position (rear) in left foot forward back stance, right hand inner middle block.

11) Turn 180° to the right on both heels (facing L3) into right foot forward back stance, right hand outer middle block (palm of fist facing front).

12A) Left foot front kick,

12B) returning foot to original position (rear) in right foot forward back stance, left hand inner middle block.

13) Look left. Turn 90° to the left on ball of right foot (facing S) stepping into left foot forward front stance, executing right hand swallow form knife-hand strike.

14A) Right foot (rear) front kick,

14B) landing foot forward in right front stance, executing a right hand back-fist to face.

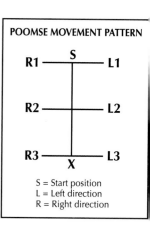

POOMSE MOVEMENT PATTERN

S = Start position
L = Left direction
R = Right direction

Taegeuk Sa Jang (4 jang)

POOMSE MOVEMENT PATTERN

```
        S
R1 ————————— L1
   |
   |
R2 ————————— L2
   |
   |
R3 ————————— L3
        X
```

S = Start position
L = Left direction
R = Right direction

15) Turn 90° to the left (facing R2) turning on ball of right foot, stepping into left walking stance, left hand inner middle block.

16) Execute right hand reverse middle punch without stepping.

17) Turn 180° to the right (facing L2), pivoting on the heels of both feet, into a right walking stance, right hand inner middle block.

18) Execute left hand reverse middle punch without stepping.

Taegeuk Sa Jang (4 jang)

19A) Turn 90° to the left (facing S) on the ball of the right foot, stepping into left front stance, left hand inner middle block,

19B) then immediately execute right hand reverse middle punch,

19C) followed by left hand middle punch (double punch) without stepping.

Taegeuk Sa Jang (4 jang)

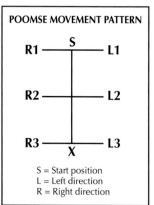

POOMSE MOVEMENT PATTERN

R1 ——— S ——— L1

R2 ——————— L2

R3 ——— X ——— L3

S = Start position
L = Left direction
R = Right direction

20A) Step right foot forward into right front stance, right hand inner middle block,

20B) immediately followed by left hand reverse middle punch,

20C) followed by right hand middle punch (double punch) without stepping. **Keeyup!**

Bahrote. Bring left foot back 180° to the rear (facing X) to start position. Sho. Kyung neh.

Taegeuk Sa Jang (4 jang)

Taegeuk Oh Jang (5 jang), 4th Gup

This Poomse is represented by the trigram "Son" (comprised of a solid upper and middle bar and a broken lower bar) which represents the wind; possessing a mighty force or calmness depending on its strength or weakness.

Charyeot. Kyung neh. Poomse Taegeuk Oh Jang. Jhoom-be. Si-jack!

1) Look left. Step left foot 90° to the left (facing L1) into left front stance, left hand down block.

2) With right foot fixed, return left foot close to right foot into natural stance (facing X). Look left. Circle left hand low and wide in front of your body, swinging overhead into a left hand down striking outside hammer-fist to your left side. Keep right hand chambered on your right hip.

3) Turn 90° to the right (facing R1) on the ball of your left foot, stepping into a right front stance, right hand down block.

4) With left foot fixed, return right foot close to left foot into natural stance (facing X). Look right. Circle right hand low and wide in front of your body, swinging overhead into a right hand down striking outside hammer-fist to your right side. Again, keeping left hand chambered on left hip.

Taegeuk Oh Jang (5 jang)

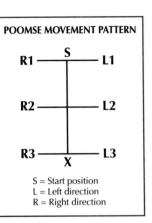

POOMSE MOVEMENT PATTERN

S = Start position
L = Left direction
R = Right direction

5A) Fix right foot, and step left foot forward (facing X) into left front stance, and execute left hand inner middle block,

5B) followed immediately with right hand inner middle block without stepping.

6A) Right foot (rear) front kick,

6B) landing to front in right front stance, executing right hand back-fist strike to the face,

6C) followed immediately with a left hand inner middle block without stepping.

Taegeuk Oh Jang (5 jang)

7A) Left foot (rear) front kick,

7B) landing to front in left front stance, executing left hand back-fist strike to face,

7C) followed immediately with a right hand inner middle block without stepping.

 8) Step right foot forward into right front stance, executing right back-fist to face.

9) Look left. Turn to the left 270° (facing R3) to the rear on the ball of your right foot into left foot forward back stance, executing left single knife-hand block.

10) Step right foot forward into right front stance, executing right elbow strike to face, left hand supporting and covering right fist.

11) Turn 180° to the right (facing L3) on the ball of the left foot, stepping into right foot front back stance, and execute right single knife-hand middle block.

12) Step left foot forward into left front stance, executing left elbow strike to face, right hand supporting and covering left fist.

Taegeuk Oh Jang (5 jang)

13A) Turn 90° to the left (facing S) on ball of right foot, stepping into left front stance, left hand down block,

13B) followed immediately by right hand inner middle block without stepping.

14A) Right foot (rear) front kick,

14B) landing forward into right front stance, right hand down block,

14C) followed immediately by left hand inner middle block without stepping.

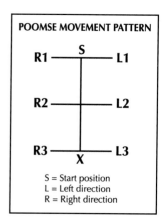

POOMSE MOVEMENT PATTERN

```
        S
R1 ———————— L1

R2 ———————— L2

R3 ———————— L3
        X
```

S = Start position
L = Left direction
R = Right direction

13A

13B

14A

14B

14C

15) Turn 90° to the left (facing R2) on ball of right foot, stepping into left front stance, left hand rising block.

16A) Execute right (rear) leg sidekick,

16B) landing in right front stance, and execute left elbow strike to face, using right palm as striking target.

17) Turn 180° to the right (facing L2) on ball of left foot stepping into right front stance, executing right rising block.

18A) Left (rear) leg sidekick,

18B) landing forward into left front stance, executing right elbow strike to face, using left palm as strike target.

Taegeuk Oh Jang (5 jang)

19A) Turn 90° to the left (facing S) on ball of right foot into left front stance, left hand down block,

19B) then right hand inner middle block without stepping.

20A) Right foot (rear) front kick,

20B) then hop forward into an X-stance (left foot crossing behind right foot) and execute right hand back-fist to face. **Keeyup!**

Bahrote. Turn your body to the left (facing X) and bring the left foot 90° to your left to start position Sho. Kyung neh.

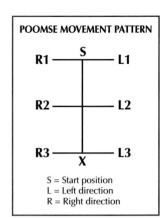

POOMSE MOVEMENT PATTERN

```
        S
R1 ─────┼───── L1
        │
R2 ─────┼───── L2
        │
R3 ─────┼───── L3
        X
```

S = Start position
L = Left direction
R = Right direction

Taegeuk Oh Jang (5 jang)

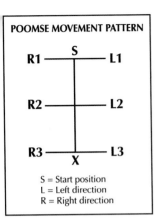

POOMSE MOVEMENT PATTERN

R1 ——— S ——— L1

R2 ——— L2

R3 ——— X ——— L3

S = Start position
L = Left direction
R = Right direction

Taegeuk Yook Jang (6 jang), 3rd Gup

This Poomse is represented by the "Kam"" (comprised of a broken upper and lower bar, and a solid middle bar), which represents water, and means incessant flow and softness.

Charyeot. Kyung neh. Poomse Taegeuk Yook Jang. Jhoom-be. Si-jack!

1) Look left. Step 90° to the left (facing L1) into left front stance, left hand down block.

2A) Right (rear) foot front kick,

2B) returning leg to original place but in left foot forward back stance, left hand outer middle block (palm facing front).

3) Turn 180° to right (facing R1) on ball of left foot, stepping into right front stance, right hand down block.

4A) Left foot (rear) front kick,

4B) returning leg to rear in original place with right foot to front in back stance, left hand outer middle block (palm facing front).

5) Turn 90° to the left (facing X) on ball of right foot, stepping into left front stance, right hand single knife-hand outside block, body slightly twisted to the left.

6) Right foot (rear) roundhouse kick to front, briefly holding knee up after kicking, then setting to the ground slightly in front.

Taegeuk Yook Jang (6 jang)

7A) Turn 90° to the left (facing L2) with right foot fixed, stepping into left front stance, left hand high outer block (palm facing front).

7B) Followed immediately by right hand reverse middle punch without stepping.

8A) Right foot (rear) front kick,

8B) landing forward in right front stance, left hand reverse middle punch.

Taegeuk Yook Jang (6 jang)

9A) Turn 180° to the right (facing R2) on ball of left foot, landing in right front stance, execute right hand high outer block (palm facing front).

9B) Followed immediately by a left hand reverse middle punch without stepping.

10A) Left foot (rear) front kick,

10B) landing forward in left front stance, right hand reverse middle punch.

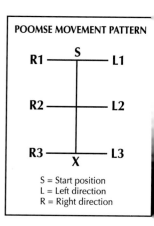

POOMSE MOVEMENT PATTERN

S = Start position
L = Left direction
R = Right direction

Taegeuk Yook Jang (6 jang)

11A) Turn 90° to the left on ball of right foot (facing X), stepping into Jhoom-be stance, cross wrists by shoulders.

11B) Then execute double hand spreading block (double low block to sides).

12) Step right foot forward into right front stance, left hand outside single knife-hand block, body slightly twisted to the right.

13) Left foot (rear) roundhouse kick. **Keeyup!** Land in left front stance.

Taegeuk Yook Jang (6 jang)

14) Turn 270° to the right (facing L3) on ball of left foot, landing in right front stance, right hand down block.

15A) Left foot (rear) front kick,

15B) returning to rear in original foot position, right foot front in back stance, right hand outer middle block (palm facing front).

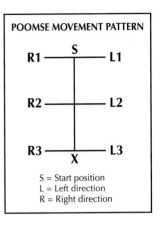

POOMSE MOVEMENT PATTERN

S = Start position
L = Left direction
R = Right direction

Taegeuk Yook Jang (6 jang)

16) Turn 180° to the left (facing R3) on the ball of the right foot, into left front stance, left hand down block.

17A) Right foot front kick,

17B) returning foot to rear in original foot position, left foot front back stance, left hand outer middle block (palm facing front).

18) Turn 90° to the left on ball of left foot (towards S, body facing X), stepping right foot to the rear into left foot forward back stance, double middle knife-hand block.

19) Step left foot to rear (towards S, body facing X) in right foot front back stance, right hand double middle knife-hand block.

Taegeuk Yook Jang (6 jang)

20) Step right foot far to rear (towards S, body still facing X) into left front stance, and execute left hand inner palm pressing block.

21) Execute right hand reverse middle punch without stepping.

22) Step left foot far to rear (towards S, body facing X) landing in right front stance, and execute right hand inner palm pressing block.

23) Execute left hand reverse middle punch without stepping. Poomse ends facing (facing X) front direction.

Bahrote. Pull right foot to rear (towards S, still facing X) into Jhoom be stance. Sho. Kyung neh.

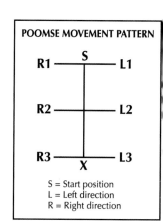

POOMSE MOVEMENT PATTERN

R1 —— S —— L1

R2 —————— L2

R3 —— X —— L3

S = Start position
L = Left direction
R = Right direction

Taegeuk Yook Jang (6 jang)

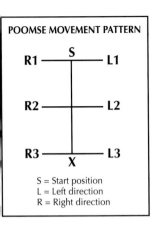

```
POOMSE MOVEMENT PATTERN

R1 ——— S ——— L1

R2 ——————— L2

R3 ——— X ——— L3

S = Start position
L = Left direction
R = Right direction
```

Taegeuk Chil Jang (7 jang), 2nd Gup

This Poomse is represented by the trigram "Kan" (comprised of a solid upper bar, and a broken middle and lower bar) which represents the mountains, meaning to ponder and firmness.

Charyeot. Kyung neh. Poomse Taegeuk Chil Jang. Jhoom-be. Si-jack!

1) Look left. Turn 90° to the left (facing L1), stepping left foot into left tiger stance, executing right hand inner middle palm block.

2A) Right (rear) foot front kick,

2B) returning it to rear in original place in left foot front tiger stance, and execute left hand inner middle block.

3) Turn 180° to the right (facing R1) on the ball of the left foot, stepping into right foot front tiger stance, and executing left hand inner middle palm block.

4A) Left foot (rear) front kick,

4B) returning it to the rear in original position in right foot front tiger stance, and execute right hand inner middle block.

5) Turn 90° to the left (facing X) on the ball of the right foot, stepping into left foot front back stance, and execute double knife-hand low block.

6) Step right foot forward into right foot front back stance, and execute double knife-hand low block.

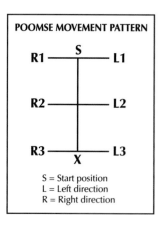

POOMSE MOVEMENT PATTERN

S = Start position
L = Left direction
R = Right direction

7) Turn 90° left (facing L2) on ball of right foot, into left foot front tiger stance, and execute right inner assisted middle palm block, left fist under right elbow (palm facing down).

8) Without stepping, execute assisted right back-fist strike to face (left fist still supporting under elbow).

9) Turn 180° to the right (facing R2) on ball of left foot, stepping into right foot front tiger stance, and execute left assisted inner middle palm block, right fist under left elbow (palm facing down).

10) Without stepping, execute assisted left back-fist strike to face (right fist still supporting under elbow).

Taegeuk Chil Jang (7 jang)

11) Bring left foot next to right foot in attention stance (facing X), left hand covering right fist and held just below the chin.

12A) Step left foot forward into left front stance, and execute left hand up scissors block.

12B) Followed immediately by a right hand up scissors block without stepping.

13A) Step right foot forward into right front stance, and execute right hand up scissors block.

13B) Followed immediately by a left hand up scissors block without stepping.

14) Turn 270° to the left (facing R3) on ball of right foot, into left front stance, execute double forearm middle spreading block (palms front).

15A) Open hands for head grab,

15B) raise the right knee up, and sharply pull both hands down to both sides of the raised knee.

15C) Step right foot forward, placing ball of left foot behind and across right foot into X-stance, and execute double uppercut to midsection.

16) With right foot fixed, slide left foot far to rear into right front stance and execute low X-block.

Taegeuk Chil Jang (7 jang)

17) Turn 180° to the right (facing L3) on ball of left foot, into right front stance, and execute double forearm middle spreading block (palms front).

18A) Open hands for head grab,

18B) raise the left knee up, and sharply pull both fists down to either side of raised knee.

18C) Step left foot forward, placing the ball of the right foot behind and across the left foot into an X-stance, and execute double uppercut to midsection.

19) With left foot fixed, slide right foot far back into left front stance, and execute low X-block.

POOMSE MOVEMENT PATTERN

R1 ——— S ——— L1

R2 ——————— L2

R3 ——— X ——— L3

S = Start position
L = Left direction
R = Right direction

Taegeuk Chil Jang (7 jang)

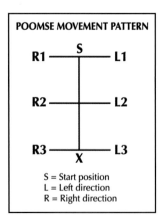

POOMSE MOVEMENT PATTERN

```
R1 ——— S ——— L1
        |
R2 ——————————— L2
        |
R3 ——— X ——— L3
```

S = Start position
L = Left direction
R = Right direction

20) Turn 90° to the left on ball of right foot (facing S), stepping into left walking stance, and execute a left back-fist to side of face.

21A) With left arm still extended after back-fist, open hand

21B) and execute right (rear) crescent/target kick to open left palm.

21C) Land right foot to front in side standing horse riding stance (body facing R2, moving towards S), striking left palm with right elbow strike.

Taegeuk Chil Jang (7 jang)

22) Turn to face start point on heel of right foot, bringing left foot up behind into right walking stance (facing S), and execute right hand back-fist to side of face.

23A) With right arm still extended, open hand, and execute left (rear) crescent/target kick to open right palm.

23B) Land left foot to front in side standing horse riding stance (body facing L2, moving towards S) striking right palm with left elbow strike.

24) With feet fixed in horse stance, execute left hand single knife-hand block.

25) Step right foot forward (facing S) and turning torso 180° (body facing R1) and execute stepping horse riding stance (towards S), and right hand side punch. **Keeyup!**

Bahrote. Turn left 90° (facing X) on ball of right foot, and return to start position, Sho. Kyung neh.

Taegeuk Chil Jang (7 jang)

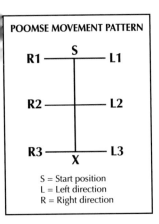

POOMSE MOVEMENT PATTERN

R1 —— S —— L1

R2 ——————— L2

R3 —— X —— L3

S = Start position
L = Left direction
R = Right direction

Taegeuk Pal Jang (8 jang), 1st Gup

This Poomse is represented by the trigram "Kon" (three broken bars), which represents Yin and the earth, meaning the root and settlement. It also represents the beginning and the end.

Charyeot. Kyung neh. Poomse Taegeuk Pal Jang. Jhoom-be. Si-jack!

1A) Step left foot forward (facing X) into back stance. Execute double fist middle block, left hand palm front, right hand palm up.

1B) Slide the left foot into front stance, execute right hand reverse middle punch.

2A) Execute left leg jumping front kick,

Taegeuk Pal Jang (8 jang)

2B) landing in left front stance, and executing left hand inner middle block,

2C) followed immediately by right hand reverse middle punch without stepping.

2D) Follow with left hand middle punch without stepping. (Kick, block, double punch).

3) Step right foot forward into right front stance, execute right hand middle punch.

4) Turn 90° to the left, pivoting on ball of right foot in right front stance (feet point towards L3), and execute right hand single mountain block, left hand down block. Eyes look to your rear (away from your front stance, facing R3)

5) Pivot to the left on ball of right foot into a left front stance (facing R3). Extend left hand and grab, pulling to right shoulder, and execute a right hand uppercut.

6A) Pivot on the right foot 90° to the right (facing L3), left foot crossing in front, and step into X-stance.

6B) Immediately step right foot to your right, pivoting 90° to the left on your right foot into left front stance (feet point towards R3), and execute left hand single mountain block, right hand down block, looking to your rear (away from front stance, towards L3).

7) Pivot on left foot into a right front stance (facing L3), extend right hand and grab, pulling to left shoulder, then execute a left uppercut.

Taegeuk Pal Jang (8 jang)

8) Look left. Turn 270° to the left on the ball of the left foot (facing x), stepping right foot to the rear into a left foot front back stance. Execute double knife-hand middle block.

9) Slide left foot into left front stance, execute right hand reverse middle punch.

10A) Right (rear) leg front kick,

10B) landing right foot slightly behind left foot. Step left foot back, pulling right foot back slightly into right tiger stance,

10C) executing a slow motion right hand inner palm block.

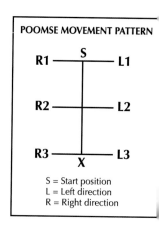

POOMSE MOVEMENT PATTERN

R1 —— **S** —— L1

R2 ———————— L2

R3 —— **X** —— L3

S = Start position
L = Left direction
R = Right direction

Taegeuk Pal Jang (8 jang)

11) With right foot fixed, turn 90° to left (facing L2), bringing left foot back slightly into left tiger stance, and execute double knife-hand middle block.

12A) Left foot (front) front kick,

12B) landing forward in left front stance, and execute right hand reverse middle punch.

13) Pull left foot back into left tiger stance, execute left hand inner palm block.

Taegeuk Pal Jang (8 jang)

14) Turn 180° to the right (facing R2) on ball of right foot into right foot front tiger stance, and execute double knife-hand middle block.

15A) Execute right (front) front kick,

15B) landing forward into right front stance, and execute left hand reverse middle punch.

16) Pull right foot back into right tiger stance, executing right hand inner palm block.

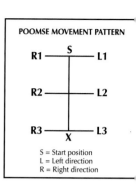

POOMSE MOVEMENT PATTERN

S = Start position
L = Left direction
R = Right direction

Taegeuk Pal Jang (8 jang)

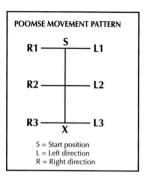

POOMSE MOVEMENT PATTERN

R1 ——— S ——— L1

R2 ——————— L2

R3 ——— X ——— L3

S = Start position
L = Left direction
R = Right direction

17) Turn on left foot to the right (facing S) into right foot front back stance, execute double fist low block.

18A) Left foot (rear) front kick

18B) and before setting it down, scissor off it and execute an in air right front kick. **Keeyup!**

18C) landing in right front stance. Immediately execute right hand inner block,

18D) followed by left hand reverse middle punch

18E) and right hand middle punch.

Taegeuk Pal Jang (8 jang)

19) Look over left shoulder. Turn 270° to the left (facing L1) on the ball of the right foot into left foot front back stance, and execute left hand single knife-hand middle block.

20) Slide left foot into left front stance, and execute unsupported right elbow strike.

21A) Execute right hand back-fist to face without stepping,

21B) followed immediately by left middle punch.

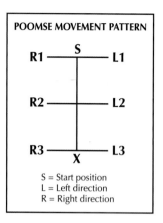

POOMSE MOVEMENT PATTERN

R1 ——— S ——— L1

R2 ——————— L2

R3 ——— X ——— L3

S = Start position
L = Left direction
R = Right direction

22) Turn 180° to the right (facing R1) off the left foot into right foot front back stance, execute right hand single knife-hand middle block.

23) Slide right foot into right front stance, and execute unsupported left elbow strike.

24A) Immediately execute left back-fist strike to face,

24B) followed immediately by right middle punch.

Bahrote. Step left foot back 90° to the left (facing X) to the start position. Sho. Kyung neh.

Taegeuk Pal Jang (8 jang)

KORYO, Probation Black Belt Poomse

The Koryo Poomse symbolizes the high spirit of the Korean people. Koryo is the ancient name of Korea, dating from the Koryo Dynasty (918 CE – 1392 CE). It was during this period that the Korean people successfully defended against the Mongol attempt to conquer their lands. Koryo Poomse should be executed with spirit and conviction, just as the Korean peoples showed during the defense of their nation.

Charyeot. Kyung neh. Poomse Koryo, Jhoom-be. (Jhoom-be for Koryo begins in the concentration thrust position, or Tong Milgi Jhoom Be.) Si-jack!

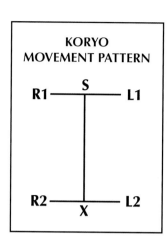

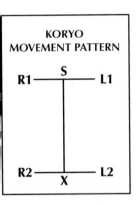

KORYO
MOVEMENT PATTERN

1) Look left. Step left foot 90° to left (facing L1) into left foot forward back stance, double knife-hand middle block.

2A) Right foot (rear) executes low sidekick,

2B) followed, without putting the leg down, by middle sidekick,

2C) landing right foot to front in right front stance, then executing right hand reverse knife-hand strike to neck (palm down).

3) Execute left hand reverse middle punch without stepping.

4) Pull right foot back into right foot front back stance, and execute right hand inner middle block.

5) Turn 180° to the right (facing R1) on ball of left foot into right foot front back stance, and execute double knife-hand middle block.

6A) Execute left foot (rear) low sidekick,

6B) followed, without putting the leg down, by middle sidekick

6C) landing foot forward in left front stance, and execute left reverse knife-hand strike to neck (palm down).

7) Followed immediately with right hand reverse middle punch without stepping.

8) Pull left foot back into left foot front back stance, and execute a left inner middle block.

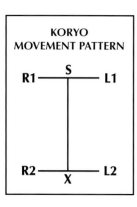

KORYO MOVEMENT PATTERN

9A) Turn 90° to the left (facing X) on ball of right foot into left front stance and execute left hand knife-hand low block,

9B) followed by right arc hand strike to throat.

10A) Right foot (rear) front kick,

10B) landing forward into right front stance, right knife-hand low block,

10C) followed immediately with left arc-hand strike to throat.

11A) Left foot (rear) front kick,

11B) landing forward to left front stance, left knife-hand low block,

11C) followed immediately with right arc-hand to throat.

12A) Right foot (rear) front kick,

12B) landing forward into right front stance. Execute a knee break by
    sweeping the right hand palm up under the leg, while executing
    a down thrusting left arc-hand to knee. **Keeyup!**

13) With right foot fixed, step left foot forward and turn 180° to the right (facing S) on ball of right foot (facing S) into right front stance, and execute double forearm wedging block (palms up).

14A) Left foot (front) front kick,

14B) landing forward in left front stance. Execute knee break by sweeping the left hand palm up under the leg, while simultaneously striking with a down thrusting right arc-hand to knee.

15) Pull left foot back in to left walking stance, executing double forearm wedging block (palms up).

16) Step right foot back 90° to the right into left foot forward back stance (body facing X, eyes facing L2) and execute outer left single knife-hand block, right fist chambered on right hip.

17) Open left palm and raise hand by bringing it around to left shoulder, and execute right hand cross body punch to open palm as target.

18A) Step right foot over in front of left foot (towards L2) into a right X-stance,

18B) and execute left foot side-kick with left hand side punch (towards L2).

18C) Land left foot in direction of kick, but step-turn the body 180° to the right (facing R2) into right front stance, and execute left spear-hand thrust to groin (palm up), while bringing right palm hand open to left shoulder.

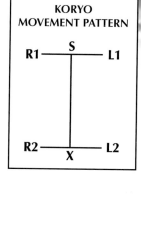

KORYO MOVEMENT PATTERN

```
R1 ——— S ——— L1
        |
        |
R2 ——— X ——— L2
```

Koryo

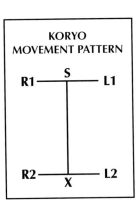

KORYO MOVEMENT PATTERN

19) Groin grab with left hand and pull left fist to hip while pulling right foot a half step back into walking stance, right hand down block.

20A) Step left foot forward (facing R2) into left foot forward walking stance, while executing left hand middle palm down pressing block.

20B) Immediately, right foot steps forward into horse riding stance (body faces X, eyes face R2) while executing right side striking elbow supported by left palm over right fist.

21) Shift feet into right foot front back stance, execute single right knife-hand middle block to right side, while chambering left hand to left hip.

22) With fixed feet, open right palm and raise hand by bringing it around to right shoulder, and execute left hand cross body punch to open palm as target.

23A) Step left foot over and in front of right foot (towards R2) into a left X-stance,

23B) and execute a right foot sidekick with right hand side punch (towards R2).

23C) Land right foot in direction of kick, but step-turn the body 180° to the left (facing L2) into a left front stance, and execute a right spear-hand thrust to the groin (palm up), while bringing left palm open to right shoulder.

24) Groin grab with right hand and pull right fist to hip while stepping left foot a half step back into left walking stance, left hand down block.

25A) Step right foot forward into walking stance, execute right hand middle palm down pressing block.

25B) Step left foot forward into horse riding stance (body faces X, eyes face L2) while executing left side striking elbow supported by right palm over left fist.

26A)	Bring right foot to left foot (facing X) in attention stance. Bring both hands from below waist to overhead while inhaling deeply,

26B)	then slowly lowering them in an outstretched circle while exhaling slowly, and then executing a left hammer fist to the right open palm as the target.

27A)	Turn 180° to the left (facing S) on the ball of right foot, stepping into left front stance (facing S) and execute left reverse knife-hand strike to neck,

27B)	followed immediately by reverse left knife-hand low block, without stepping.

28A) Right foot steps forward into right front stance, execute right inside knife-hand strike to neck,

28B) followed by right reverse knife-hand low block.

29A) Left foot steps forward into left front stance, execute left inside knife-hand to neck,

29B) followed by left reverse knife-hand low block.

30) Right foot steps forward into right front stance, execute right arc-hand to throat. **Keeyup!**

Bahrote. Turn 180° to the left (facing X) on ball of right foot to original start position. Execute concentration thrust. Sho. Kyung neh.

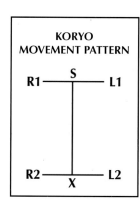

KORYO
MOVEMENT PATTERN

Koryo

BREAKING TECHNIQUES (KYUK PAH)

The **purposes** of breaking techniques are to build confidence, and to demonstrate your abilities and proper technique. It is a demonstration of your power and determination as a Tae Kwon Do stylist. Your success in executing a break is a celebration of this accomplishment. It is a reward in itself to know that you possess this ability, and are capable of showing this skill to others. You will be required to break boards at every testing level in order to advance to the next belt. Just like every other aspect of Tae Kwon Do, you will start with a basic technique, a snapping front kick, and progress to more advanced techniques, such as jump spin kicks and perhaps even multiple breaks.

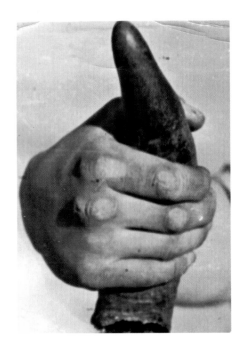

CAUTION! Breaking boards or any other material can cause injury to yourself and the board holder(s). Breaks should never be performed without proper supervision and coaching. Children and young people must be especially careful. Your bones are still growing, and because of this, they are still soft. They will harden once you finish growing. Until then, avoid most hand breaks. Your feet are more naturally conditioned because you walk and run on them. They have thick skin and have become acclimated to some pounding. The bones in your hands need to be protected, so if you must perform breaks with them, execute techniques that use the naturally toughest and best protected parts of your hand, such as the hammer-fist, knife-hand or palm heel for breaks. Avoid actively conditioning your hands for breaking until you are at least 18 years of age. Young people should not do knuckle breaks, or any break that will injure their hand. Children may practice striking soft targets like pads or paddles. Break-away boards made of plastic that split down the middle are a good tool to use and helps avoid injury.

Breaking as a science is a complete body of accumulated and organized knowledge. Overall, Tae Kwon Do is a scientific approach to the attacks and counter attacks by another human being. However, breaking has its own set of rules and preparation, and it starts with conditioning. Conditioning is for those who wish to progress to more difficult breaks, and is only appropriate for adults. The conditioning begins with daily impact training. To prepare our hands for breaks, we must pre-condition them to avoid injury. There are several ways to condition for breaking, but the end result of this training increases your bone density and, through regular exercises, gradually desensitizes the hand.

Some of you may be recalling the old adage referring to brick breaking techniques that "bricks don't hit back!" Well that is true in and of itself. But when push comes to shove, would you prefer to get hit by a person who does kickboxing aerobics, or someone who breaks rocks with his bare hands? Being able to break stacks of boards or bricks with a single blow is an obvious and valuable skill for any martial artist.

The history of breaking is part folklore, part rumor, part fiction and part fact. Considering the many different styles of Martial Arts, the variations and materials used over the centuries for breaking runs the gamut from paper to steel, including wood, earthenware, brick, stone, glass, concrete, ice, coconuts, melons, and everything in between. There are stories about Masters killing tigers with their bare hands. Mas Oyama knocked horns off charging Mexican bulls. Tae Kwon Do breaking techniques are as varied as they are impressive. They are performed with the hands, feet, elbows, shins, knees, forearms, shoulders and the head. Mostly though, we just use our hands, elbows and feet.

In the Dojang and as a color belt you will only break boards. As a black belt you will break concrete blocks. Injuries may unfortunately occur just like they can in any sport. Sometimes the injury may occur in the Dojang, at a tournament or during an exhibition. Once you are injured, really injured, not just bruised or banged up a little, immediately stop your activity and check it out. The exhilaration we feel and the adrenaline that pumps through our veins can mask a serious injury. People with broken limbs should not continue to fight, even if they think they can. Breakers who have injured themselves are subject to the same restraint. It is possible to ignore a broken bone in a hand or foot until an event is over, provided that you're tough enough, but you should not continue. Your life is not at stake, and you will live to break or compete another day. Possessing the indomitable spirit is extremely important, but don't be thick headed about your health and safety.

Breaking requirements for belt testing are as follows:

9th Gup, White Belt   none required
8th Gup, Yellow Belt   Front kick with ball of foot (Fig. 1)

7th Gup, Orange Belt   Roundhouse kick with ball of foot (Fig. 2)

6th Gup, Green Belt   Skipping sidekick with heel of foot (Fig. 3)

5th Gup, Purple Belt   Axe kick (Fig. 4)

4th Gup, Blue Belt   Jumping front kick (Fig. 5)

3rd Gup, Brown Belt   Back kick (Fig. 6)

2nd Gup, Red Belt, Low   Flying sidekick or jump spinning hook kick (shown) (Fig. 7)

1st Gup, Red Belt, High   Jump turning back sidekick and a speed break opposite hand for adults (shown) (Fig. 8, 9)

Deputy Black Belt   Hammer-fist, knife-hand or palm heel break of concrete blocks for adults (shown), (Fig. 10, 11)
Wooden boards for children, hammer-fist, palm heel or knife-hand

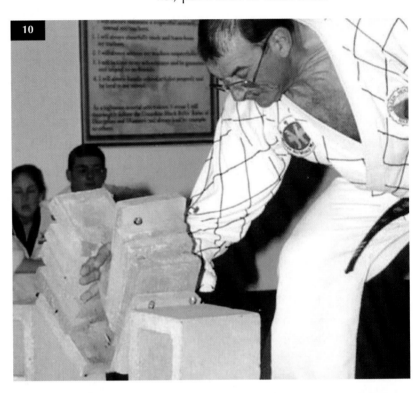

Senior Black Belts   One concrete block per belt level
First degree breaks one concrete block.
Second Dan breaks two blocks, third Dan
breaks three blocks, etc. (Fig. 12)

All your breaking techniques will start and end in the formal manner. When called to make your break, present yourself at attention. Bow, and approach your breaking station, or board holder(s). Bow to holder(s), and when instructed, prepare yourself for the break. Focus, only seeing your target. Focus on a small target, so you strike with precision. You are allowed to measure your distance or practice with no contact to your board. When ready, advise your board holder(s), take in your breath, and execute your break fast and powerfully, with a loud Keeyup. Immediately return to your starting position, bow to holder(s) and Masters, and collect your broken boards. Do as instructed from that time until your test is completed.

SPARRING AND TECHNIQUES

Sparring is one of Tae Kwon Do's ultimate objectives. It combines elements from your basics, kicking combinations, Poomse, and one-step self defense techniques. There are different styles of sparring, with each one having a different objective.

Practical sparring is used in a defensive situation to protect yourself, your family or your companions if threatened. There are no target areas you are confined to hit, in contrast to Olympic sparring, and it is acceptable to use any amount of reasonable force and any technique of which you have knowledge. There are no "legal" areas, and your only limitation in defending is good judgment. Your goal is strictly to protect yourself and disable your attacker.

Olympic and tournament sparring is for competition, and there are clearly set rules you must follow and specific target areas that you are allowed to attack.

Exhibition sparring is for demonstration purposes and allows the audience to see the ebb and flow of attacks and defenses for entertainment purposes. No contact is usually made with your partner(s), but it shows the possibilities and techniques to the viewing audience.

Free sparring, and alternate free sparring, is done with a partner to practice what you have been taught and further learn how to apply your techniques. You will learn how and when to attack, defend, trap an opponent, counter attack, block, side step, check, and apply combinations effectively. You must use maximum control at all times. Your partner is your companion, colleague, and learning associate. You never want to injure your partner, or use excessive force. Save power techniques for the heavy bag or other practice drills. Never injure or unleash your power on your partner. When sparring, control your power and your emotions, and maintain mental control at all times. This will result in a safe and controlled practice environment and allow you and your partner the best possible learning opportunity.

Sparring is fast and requires you to be light on your feet. Light jumping from a natural upright stance, with rapid foot changes between front and back, is essential. We mentioned in one-step sparring techniques the open and closed stance positions. You will remember that an open stance, also known as an open sided stance, is a mirror image of your opponent's stance. Specifically, if their left foot is forward, your right foot should be forward; and conversely, if their right foot is forward, your left foot should be forward. A closed stance, also known as a closed sided stance, is a stance in which you both have either your left foot or right foot forward at the same time. It is important to be aware of your opponent's stance because that will determine your attack or counter-attack. Some spinning techniques are more effectively delivered from the closed stance (otherwise you might kick to your opponent's back, which is an illegal technique in competition). Spinning techniques from the open stance might require you to switch your feet first so that your contact will be to the front or side of your opponent.

In free sparring, the following 15 basic techniques, specifically chosen by Grandmaster Park are your starting point for the competition ring.

1) Stepping front kick, double punch.

2) Rear leg front kick, double punch, second rear leg front kick, double punch.

3) Stepping roundhouse, double punch.

4) Step spinning back kick, double punch.

5) Axe Kick, double punch (closing technique).

6) Skipping/jumping front kick, double punch.

7) Skipping sidekick.

8) Stationary wheel kick (inside to outside axe kick)

9) Spinning wheel kick.

10) Back turning jumping roundhouse.

11) Step turning jump roundhouse

12) Cut kick, stationary sidekick.

13) To defend against a roundhouse: Back turning sidekick (back kick).

14) To defend against a roundhouse: Jump turning back leg roundhouse.

15) To defend against a charge: Roundhouse.

These techniques illustrate the basics for competition sparring. The progression in which these are taught, and their purpose, is further described below.

1) Combination kicks in sparring are consecutive kicks, one after another. If performed rapidly, it is difficult to defend against a constant attack, and combinations offer a better chance of scoring points or hitting your target than does a single kick.

2) Side stepping for attacking and defending allows you to get to the outside of your opponent when least expected. Stepping out

when attacked moves you away from the line of attack. Being on the outside of your opponent, you have a defensive advantage.

3) Checking techniques, sometimes referred to as stop hits or cut kicks, can stop an attack before it fully develops. Preventing a kick gives you the opportunity to counter attack.

4) Trapping opponents with back kicks will beat an opponent to the punch. You set your opponent up and allow him or her to start their technique, but beat them to the punch by executing a fast back sidekick, or back kick, when they expose themselves.

5) Attacks with skipping kicks are a closing technique that may deceive the opponent, causing him or her to think that the incorrect leg is developing to kick. More often it is a rapid distance closing technique combined with a kick.

6) Trapping opponents with spinning hook kicks is a set up which, through your own body positioning, draws your enemy into attacking you while you counter and beat them to the punch with your spin kick. Or, you may throw a spinning hook kick, letting your leg hang in the air but chambered, so that when your opponent believes that he or she is charging in to score, they get hit with a roundhouse from the chambered leg.

7) Double kicks are executed with one or both legs. For example, it may be a left leg roundhouse, followed immediately by a jumping right leg roundhouse. Or, as another example, it may be a left leg middle roundhouse, immediately followed by a high roundhouse from the same leg.

8) Attacks using side stepping techniques without backing up allow you to step off the center line of attack, and counter while your enemy closes the distance between you. In this way, you alter the angle of attack without retreating, countering with an appropriate kick, such as roundhouse, wheel or side kick.

9) A counter attack using a side step skipping roundhouse against a back kick will remove you from the line of attack and, for an effective counter attack, align you with your attacker's open center.

Free sparring is a specialty, just like each different area of your Tae Kwon Do training. It requires continual practice and hard training to learn these skills. Speed, as well as stamina, is essential. If you can beat your opponent to the punch or kick every time, you will score points and win. Stick to your basics, develop your abilities, and build on them.

COMPETITION TAE KWON DO

Tae Kwon Do has evolved from an ancient martial art to a modern martial sport. Today, it is an Olympic sport with members from over 130 nations participating in these international games. Worldwide, there are now 60 Million practitioners, from 179 nations, training in Tae Kwon Do.

From its origin as a martial art and the early sport of Subaki, Tae Kwon Do has found popularity worldwide in an acceptable form of competition with rules and equipment developed to protect the participants. From the first World Taekwondo Federation (WTF) international competition in 1973 in Seoul, Korea, a basis for competition rules were formed and equipment was introduced that allowed hard contact without the likelihood of serious injury. Olympic competition is limited to sparring (Gyroogi). But there are hundreds of other tournaments that allow participants to compete in forms, weapons and breaking, all integral parts of Tae Kwon Do training.

Olympic sparring has become a sophisticated event with highly talented athletes competing from all around the globe. Although Korean in origin, Tae Kwon Do now belongs to the world, thanks to the teachings of many great Masters and their lifetime of dedication. Tae Kwon Do in the Dojang looks very different from Tae Kwon Do in the competition ring. This is only natural, as the target areas we use in self defense are prohibited techniques in the ring. Competition is the sport aspect, and with limited target areas for necessities sake, the objectives are different, and this affects the overall appearance of the art. However, this limited version of Tae Kwon Do is exciting to watch. It is lightening fast, explosive, aero-acrobatic and highly refined in its complexity of techniques.

The World Taekwondo Federation has instituted a universal set of **competition rules** that allow competitors worldwide to compete on an equal footing. The competition ring measures 10 meters by 10 meters.

There are 4 judges and one referee, as well as a ring doctor and recorder. Competitors wear red or blue for differentiation in the ring, and have their coach present at ringside. Location and positions of judges, coaches, recorder and doctors are all specified in the competition rules.

The uniforms worn by competitors are Tae Kwon Do uniforms. Protective gear must include a trunk (chest & rib) protector, head protector, groin guard, forearm guards, shin guards, gloves and a mouthpiece. Groin, forearm and shin guards must be worn underneath the uniform. All equipment must be WTF approved.

Competitors participating in WTF or IOC (International Olympic

Committee) events are subject to testing for banned substances before competitions.

Weight classes are divided into men' and women's divisions. There are eight divisions for WTF and five for Olympic competition. Weight divisions for Junior World Championships are divided into 10 categories. Team competitions are also divided into weight classifications. Competitions are conducted in two different ways, single elimination and round robin. Olympic competition is conducted strictly on an individual basis.

All contests will consist of three two-minute rounds, with a one-minute rest between rounds. In the event of a tie after the third round, a fourth round of two minutes will be conducted as the sudden death overtime round.

Drawing lots will determine competition orders and weigh-in of competitors will be conducted in accordance with the rules as outlined, the day before competitions. Competitors will be called to the ring and must appear in the ring within one minute of the competition. They will then undergo a physical inspection and costume inspection before the bout begins. After inspection, competitors will enter into the waiting position with one coach.

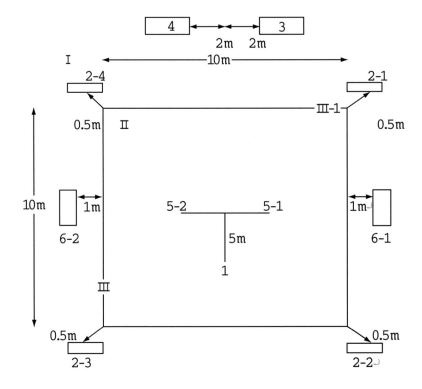

Contests start with the command "Si-jak" (start) by the referee, and end with "Keu-man" (stop).

The procedure before and after the end of the contest is as follows. Competitors face each other at attention and bow. Referee starts the competition by commanding "Jhoom-Be" (ready) and "Si-jak" (start). At the end of the last round, competitors will face each other standing in their respective positions and the referee will command "Charyeot'" (attention) and "Kyung neh" (bow), and then wait for the referee's declaration of the decision. The referee will declare the winner by raising his hand to the winner's side.

Techniques permitted are with either the fist or the foot. Fist techniques must be delivered with the front parts of the forefinger and middle finger of a tightly clenched fist. Foot techniques must be delivered using the parts of the foot below the ankle.

Areas permitted to strike are the trunk of the body on areas protected by the trunk guard, but not to the back where the guard does not protect the body. When attacking the face, the competitor is only permitted to use his feet, and can target only the front and the area protected by the head guard, except the back of the head. No hand techniques are allowed to the head or face.

Scoring areas are to the mid-section of the trunk, the abdomen and both sides of the flank, and permitted areas of the face. Points are awarded when permitted techniques are delivered accurately and powerfully to the legal scoring areas. A competitor earns one point for an attack on the chest protector, and two points for techniques to face. An additional one point is scored for a legal knockdown in which the referee counts. Winner is the competitor with the most total points for three rounds.

Points can be invalidated by a competitor falling intentionally, immediately after delivering a legitimate technique, by delivering an illegal technique after delivering a scoring legal technique, or by performing any of the prohibited actions.

The referee declares penalties for any prohibited acts. Penalties are divided into warnings (Kyung-Go) and deductions (Gam-geum). Two warnings result in a one-point deduction. A deduction call results in a one-point deduction. "Odd Warnings" do not accumulate or count in the final points total.

Kyung-Go warning penalties for prohibited acts are as follows:
1) Crossing the boundary line.
2) Evading by turning the back to an opponent.
3) Falling down.

4) Avoiding the match.

5) Grabbing, holding or pushing an opponent.

6) Attacking below the waist.

7) Pretending to be injured.

8) Butting or attacking with knees.

9) Hitting an opponent's face with hand.

10) Undesirable utterances or remarks, or any misconduct on the part of a competitor or a coach.

Gam-geum deductions shall be declared for the following acts defined as prohibited:

1) Attacking an opponent after referee declares "Kal-yeo" (break).

2) Attacking a fallen opponent.

3) Throwing down an opponent by grabbing their attacking foot in the air with your arm, or by pushing the opponent with your hand.

4) Intentionally attacking an opponent's face with your hand.

5) A coach or competitor interrupting the progress of the match.

6) Violent or extreme remarks or behavior on the part of a contestant or a coach.

When a competitor intentionally refuses to comply with the competition rules or the referee's orders, the referee may declare that competitor the loser by penalty after one minute. When a competitor receives four deduction points, the referee shall declare him/her loser due to penalties. Warning and deduction points shall be counted in the total score of the three rounds.

Decisions are declared as follows:

1) Win by knockout (K.O.).

2) Win because Referee Stops Contest (RSC).

3) Win by score or superiority:

a) Win by final score.

b) Win by point gap: when there is a 7-point gap, the match will be stopped and the winner declared.

c) Win by point ceiling: when a competitor scores a maximum of 12-points, the match shall be stopped and the winner declared.

4) Win by withdrawal.

5) Win by disqualification.

6) Win by referee's punitive declaration.

These are the competition rules as they apply to competitors. These rules are more extensive than presented here, with specifics relating to knockdowns, referees, recorders, assignments of officials, arbitration and other matters not specified in the rules. It is a good policy to review the rules periodically so you will avoid making deductible errors.

Poomse (also known as **forms**) are an integral part of Tae Kwon Do, and it seems natural that competitions would include them along with sparring, weapons competition, and breaking techniques.

Forms competition is one of the most exciting events to watch at tournaments. It covers three main areas of performance:

1) Traditional forms

2) Competition forms

3) Musical/open forms

Traditional forms are exactly that, the Poomse or forms you were taught at your school. In Tae Kwon Do competitions, you will see all the various Poomse sets performed by one school or another. Judges take into consideration many things in determining a Poomse Champion. Among these are:

1) Correctness of the pattern

2) Proper execution

3) Grace and power

4) Breathing technique

5) Kee-yups

6) Competition etiquette

7) General appearance

Competitors perform the appropriate Poomse or Hyung for their level, as taught at their school.

Competition forms are patterns choreographed by the student or learned form another source. They may be performed in a traditional manner, but modern competition usually requires patterns and performances with more flair, more flying and acrobatic combinations, and in general, more oriented for entertainment than practicality.

Musical Poomse are forms that are performed to a chosen piece of music. The combination puts greater emphasis on the rhythm, grace and timing.

Weapons Poomse allow most weapons used by martial artists to be used in the performance of a pattern suitable for that weapon. The list is considerable, and includes the sword, staff, knife, sai, kama, and nunchuk. The limiting element is the danger posed to others, and sharpened weapons are discouraged. There are a variety of categories for weapons competition as well, and vary from event to event.

Breaking competitions are a regular event at most tournaments, although the materials permitted vary a great deal. The traditional materials used are 1" thick wooden pine boards, 2" concrete blocks, and clay bricks. Most tournaments allow a number of stations, in many cases up to four, with each competitor's break of choice. In some events, each competitor is judged by how they perform the exact same break. This could be a number of clay bricks, boards or concrete blocks stacked and broken. Creative breaking will allow you to see jump breaks, spinning breaks, hand techniques, and exotic techniques performed. It can be one of the more impressive events at any tournament.

Self defense competitions are a group performance, where one person is the intended victim, while the other players are the attackers. Usually there are two to three people attacking the victim in a pre-arranged, or choreographed, set of attacks and defenses. Skits are often a scenario, for example, where Miss Jane might be walking home from school, and three bully's attempt to do her harm. Miss Jane wards off all attacks with defensive techniques, and disables her attackers. These skits usually take two to three minutes to perform, and are a true testament to the defense capabilities taught in Tae Kwon Do.

Exhibitions (**Shibum**) and **demonstrations** have been an excellent way for interested parties, students and the general public to see Masters and students alike perform their art. From the earliest years of Tae Kwon Do's introduction into the USA, exhibitions were the way for practitioners to demonstrate their capabilities. Grandmaster Dong Kuen Park, having recently opened his school in Journal Square in Jersey City, New Jersey, performed for America's viewing audience on the Johnny Carson show in 1971.

Korea has several touring demonstration teams that perform around the world. The Korean Tigers and Hodori Demonstration teams are professional groups of superior ability that excite audiences without exception. Universities, such as Bridgeport University, Kyung Hee University and Yong-In University, have performance teams. And in most Tae Kwon Do schools there are teams that practice on a regular basis to perfect and share their joy, pride, love and accomplishment of Tae Kwon Do with the community at large.

For over thirty years, many universities and colleges in the USA have formed Tae Kwon Do clubs. As a young practitioner, you may want to continue your Tae Kwon Do studies and practice if you travel to another city or town after your high school graduation. You can still practice your art and perfect your skills as you continue your growth throughout life. Tae Kwon Do will become a part of you and a way of life. You never have to give it up, if you don't want to.

There are universities now in America, as there are in Korea and other countries around the world that offer degree programs in Tae Kwon Do. In these programs, you will study many other courses along with Tae Kwon Do, in order for you to achieve a fuller body of knowledge, become a more rounded individual, and experience many of the other disciplines of life.

Many of you readers will explore Tae Kwon Do for a year, maybe two and some longer than that. A small portion of those who start training will reach black belt. And a few of those black belts will become Masters, dedicating themselves to this valuable and fulfilling art and way of life. But every student that begins their training will learn valuable techniques and life lessons, even if they only train for a short time. What you earn and take away from it will stay with you as part of the sum total of your life experiences, and you will come away enriched—in knowledge, ability, confidence, friendship, and spirituality.

Only you, the student, can decide what you want from Tae Kwon Do. You must decide if you want to be the best martial artist you can be, or if you want to be a champion. Many dedicated black belts remain participants in Tae Kwon Do years after they've performed their last jump flying spin kick, or broken their last brick. Tae Kwon Do is a community of practitioners, and as such, you will see familiar faces at tournaments and competitions all around the nation, and the world. Judges, coaches, referees, recorders and officials are, or were practitioners at some time in their life and remain active in Tae Kwon Do. You have a rich legacy with a colorful history behind your Tae Kwon Do. Use what you have learned wisely, justly and without malice. And strive to be the best of the best.

GLOSSARY

Korean	English
Ah kum sahn	arc hand or fork hand
Ahn magkie	inside block
Ahp jung kang yi	shin
An son nal doong	ridge hand (reverse of knife-hand)
Anio	no
Ap chagie	front kick
Ap dolyo chagi	roundhouse kick
Ap goobi jhase	front stance
Ap koa seogi	X-stance, lead leg stays front
Ap kum chi	ball of foot
Ap seogi jhase	walking stance
Areh	low
Areh magkie	low block
Ba jie	pants (uniform)
Ba kat magkie	outside block
Bahrote	finish, return to ready stance
Bal da kwoe chagie	switch kick
Bal nal	blade of foot
Ban dal chagie	hook Kick
Ban deh chirugie	reverse punch
Bi kim	tie (judges ruling)
Biteuro chagi	twist kick
Bokboo	center (where Ki is generated)
Buder chagie	axe kick
Bum seogi	tiger stance
Chagie	kick
Charyeot	attention
Chigi	chop
Chirugie	punch
Chun jin	quick step forward
Chung	blue
Dan	black belt ranking (adult)/Degree
Ddweyo chagie	jumping kick
Dee ro dol gi	about face
Deung ju mok ap chigie	back-fist strike
Dhi dola hwe gun chagie	spinning wheel kick
Do	the Way
Do bok	uniform
Do jang	school
Dolmyo chagie	spinning kick
Dwit chagie	back kick
Dwit goobi jhase	back stance
Dwit koa seogi	x-stance, lead leg lands rear
Gam geum	deduction (point)
Gawi magkie	scissors block
Geodeuro areh magkie	double fist low block
Geodeuro momtong magkie	double fist middle block
Gu mon	stop
Gui	ear
Gullgi chirugie	hook punch
Gup	grade
Gwe	divination signs (tri-grams)
Gyroogi	sparring
Hae cho	class dismissed
Han bun gyrugi	one step sparring
Hansonnal mok chigi	knife-hand neck chop
Hechuh magkie	wedging blocks
Ho gu	chest protector

Hong	red	Mikulgi chagie	sliding kick
Hosin sool	self-defense	Mil a chagie	push kick
. . . .		Mok	neck
Hwe jun	round number	Mokoomeong	throat
Hwe jun chagi	wheel kick, swing, half moon, outside to inside	Momtong	middle
		Momtong chirugie	middle punch
Hyung	patterns/forms	Momtong magkie	middle block
		Moo ree	head
In joong	philtrum	Moo rup	knee
		Moa seogi	fighting stance
Jebipoom sonnal mok chigi	swallow-form knife-hand strike	Mu sul	martial skill
		Mudo	martial morality
Jhase	position (stance)	Myung chi	solar plexus
Jhoom be jhase	ready stance		
Jooi	warning	Nada bum	jump spinning roundhouse
Ju choom jhase	horse riding stance		
Ju mok	fist	Noon	eye
Ju mok chirugie	punching		
Jung shin tong il	concentration of spirit	Oe santeul magkie	single mountain block
Jwa woo hyang woo	face each other	Olgul	high
		Olgul chirugie	high punch
Kae sork	continue	Olgul magkie	high block
Kahm sa hamnida	thank you		
Kal yeo	break (sparring)	Pa tang son	palm-heel
Keeyup	loud shouting	Pa tang son an magkie	palm-heel block
Keu man	halt or stop	Pal chagie	kicking stance
Kuki yeh	facing the flags	Pal goop	elbow
Kwan jang nim	grandmaster	Pal mok	forearm
Kwon	hand	Peonee seogi	resting stance
Kya dae	switch	Poom	black belt ranking (adolescents)
Kye shi	suspend (the time keeping)		
		Poomse	forms
Kyo cha seogi	X-stance	Pyojeok chagie	target kick, crescent, outside to inside
Kyobum nim	instructor		
Kyosa nim	assistant instructor	Pyonson Keut chirugie	spear-hand thrust
Kyuk pah	breaking	Pyoogi	stretching
Kyung go	warning		
Kyung neh	bow	Sa bum nim	Master Instructor
		Sae bun chirugie	triple punch
Magkie	block	Santeul magkie	mountain block
Meh ju mok	hammer-fist	Seogi	stance
Meh ju mok chigi	hammer-fist strike	Sheo	rest or at ease
		Si jack	start

Sikan . . . . time

Son nal . . . . knife-hand

Son nal magkie. . . . . knife-hand block

Son nal mok chigie . . . . neck chop

Sonnal areh magkie . . . . double knife-hand low block

Sonnal momtong magkie . . . double knife-hand middle block

Sosum chirugie. . . . . double uppercut

Sto magkie . . . . knife-hand block

Sun bae nim . . . . Senior belt

Tae. . . . . foot

Taegukdo. . . . . Korean national flag

Toe ra . . . . about face

Tong milgi. . . . . concentration thrust

Um yang . . . . negative/positive

Uht doree . . . . jacket (uniform)

Who jin. . . . . quick step backward

Ye or ne . . . . yes

Yedan bal chagie. . . . . stepping kick

Yeot georeo magkie . . . . X-block

Yo poseyo . . . . hello

Yok son kahl . . . . ridge hand

Yup chagie . . . . sidekick

Zipap. . . . . line up

Counting

Ha na. . . . . one

Dool . . . . two

Set . . . . three

Net. . . . . four

Da sot . . . . five

Ya sot . . . . six

Il gob . . . . seven

Yo dul . . . . eight

Ah hope . . . . nine

Yul . . . . ten

Sue mul . . . . twenty

Set reun. . . . . thirty

Ma heun . . . . forty

Shi heun . . . . fifty

Eh seun . . . . sixty

Il heun. . . . . seventy

Yun deun. . . . . eighty

Ah deun . . . . ninety

Beck. . . . . hundred

Chun . . . . thousand

Man. . . . . ten thousand

Ship man. . . . . hundred thousand

Beck man . . . . million

Il. . . . . first

Ee. . . . . second

Sam . . . . third

Sa. . . . . fourth

Oh . . . . fifth

Yook. . . . . sixth

Chil . . . . seventh

Pal . . . . eighth

Goo . . . . ninth

Ship . . . . tenth

BIBLIOGRAPHY

The Random House College Dictionary, Revised Edition

The Columbia Encyclopedia, Sixth Edition, 2001

Encyclopedia Britannica

Tae Kwon Do World, Grandmaster Y.K. Kim, 1985

"Sports Nutrition" article, *American Orthopedic Society for Sports Medicine*, 2001

The World Tae Kwon Do Federation www.wtf.org

Kukkiwon Headquarters www.kukkiwon.or.kr/eng/

American Tae Kwon Do Association www.ataonline.com

Suk Jun Kim's Tae Kwon Do NYC, NY www.sjkim-taekwondo.com

Power Kix Karate www.powerkixusa.com

"People and events in Tae Kwon Do's Formative Years", Dakin Burdick, "1996, Revised 1999

"History of Tae Kwon Do" www.geocities.com/t.avery@sbcglobal.net/tkd/ tk_history.html

"Korean and Tae kwon Do History" by Ken Whitewolf www.thewhitewolf.net/ tkdhistory.html

Tae Kwon Do, Gen. Hong Hi Choi, "1972

Tae Kwon Do Hyung, Grandmaster Hee Il Cho, 1984

The Art of War, by Sun Tzu, translated Samuel B. Griffith ©1963

"Tae Kwon Do, Yesterday and Today", Master Allison Meador "1999

"The History of Tae Kwon Do" by Master Jun Lee, Article, *Tae Kwon Do Times*, March 1995

"The History of Tae kwon Do", *Hwang's Martial Arts*, www.hwangsmartialarts.com

"Korean History" by Jung Kang Yup, www.sogang.ac.kr

"History of Tae Kwon Do" source *Asian Sun*, "2004 Trinity College TKD Club

Judo, T. Shozo Kuwashima & Ashbel R. Welch 1943

Bruce Lee's Fighting Methods, Self Defense Techniques, Bruce Lee & M. Uyehara, ©1976

BIBLIOGRAPHY

Deadly Karate Blows, The Medical Implications, Brian Adams ©1985

This is Karate, Masutatsu Oyama, ©1968 Japan Publications Trading Company, Rutland, Tokyo, New York.

"History of the American Flag", www.usa-flag-site.org

"The Korean National Flag", www.itatkd.com

"South Koreas Flag", www.enchantedlearning.com

"South Korea, Symbolism of Flag", http://.fotw.fivestarflags.com

The I Ching, or Book Of Changes, Richard Wilhelm translation. Bollingen Series 19, Princeton University Press, Third Edition, 24th printing, 1990

"Martial Arts and the Law", www.members.tripod.com/~aimvtaekwondo/law.html, Further: "Martial Arts and The Law", Shihan Pat Merriman, Attorney at Law

"The Law of Self Defense in Illinois", http://pages.prodigy.net/fhattys/page10.html

Tae Kwon Do, The Ultimate reference Guide to the Worlds Most Popular Martial Art, Yeon Hee Park, Yeon Hwan Park, Jon Gerrard, ©1989, Facts On File, Inc.

The Soul Of A Butterfly; Reflections on Lifes Journey, Muhammad Ali, with Hana Yasmeen Ali, © 2004, Simon & Schuster

Tae Kwon Do; Secrets of Korean Karate, Sihak Henry Cho, Charles Tuttle and Company, ©1968, Fourth printing, 1994

Korean Intangible Cultural Properties; Traditional Music and Dance, Cultural properties Administration, Republic of Korea ©2000

Explore Korea, Essence of Culture and Tourism, published by the Ministry of Culture and Tourism, Republic of Korea, ©2001

A Modern History of Taekwondo, Kang Won Sik and Lee Kyong Myong, ©1999 Published by Bokyung Moonhwasa, Seoul, Korea

Korean Karate; The Art of Tae Kwon Do, Duk Sung Son and Robert J. Clark, ©1968 Published by Prentice-Hall, Inc.